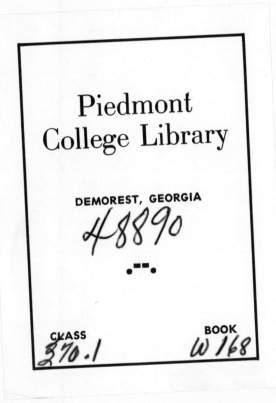

Education and
Political Power

THE LIBRARY OF EDUCATION

A Project of The Center for Applied Research in Education, Inc.

G. R. Gottschalk, Director

Categories of Coverage

I	II	III
Curriculum and Teaching	Administration, Organization, and Finance	Psychology for Educators

IV	V	VI
History, Philosophy, and Social Foundations	Professional Skills	Educational Institutions

Education and
Political Power

JOHN E. WALSH, C.S.C., PH.D.

*Vice-President, Public Relations and
Development
University of Notre Dame*

The Center for Applied Research in Education, Inc.
New York

Second Printing...February, 1967

IMPRIMI POTEST
Howard J. Kenna, C.S.C.
Provincial

NIHIL OBSTAT
Leo R. Ward, C.S.C., Ph.D.
Censor Deputatus

IMPRIMATUR
✠ Leo A. Pursley, D.D.
Bishop of Fort Wayne-South Bend

LIBRARY OF CONGRESS
CATALOG CARD NO.: 64–16040

PRINTED IN THE UNITED STATES OF AMERICA

5-1-'67 pb. 3-62

Foreword

           This book deals with one of the most important and difficult of educational problems. What is the relationship between political power and the schools? What is expected of education in a given society, and how is this expectation fulfilled? Father Walsh provides clear and thoughtful answers to these questions. First, he compares what happens in a democracy with the results of rule by one man or an elite. This sets the stage for the dominant theme: viewing the professed educational aims and methods of contemporary dictatorships, what are the chances of the democratically oriented school both in highly developed societies like our own and in those which are emerging and attempting to shape their destinies?

Father Walsh is neither a blithe optimist nor a prophet of doom. His book is an eloquent and ably reasoned argument for the democratic idea, but at the same time it makes abundantly evident that this idea must first of all be understood and then put into effect. A free society begins with an act of faith: "All men are created equal." Having so decided, it must bring the full force of reason to bear on how the implications of equality are to be realized. Insofar as education is concerned, the functions are two: the necessary knowledge must be made available to all citizens, and a value-system consonant with the nature of a free society must be taught.

Both of these statements have been widely discussed by educators, who have often enough disagreed. Father Walsh presents the various positions fairly and makes a strong case for his own views. Among the important and difficult issues dealt with are the relationship between public and private education, the status of the intellectual, training for leadership, and intercultural studies. The reader will be grateful for the fact that problems of such importance are dealt with in straightforward fashion, revealing the author's forceful personality. He will also thank this same author for not having assumed that whims, quirks, and extremist opinions are necessary in one who is writing about education.

GEORGE N. SHUSTER
Former President of Hunter College,
Assistant to the President
University of Notre Dame

Education and
Political Power

John E. Walsh, C.S.C.

Ordinarily the association of education and politics is deplored. This is because politics has come to be associated with the impact of petty and short range interests on the conduct of the schools. In a more significant sense, however, politics refers to large scale and long range public interests in the management of the schools. In this sense the mixture of education and politics amounts to educational statesmanship. Undoubtedly this is the view that Aristotle took when he wrote on education in his *Politics*. It is also the view that Father Walsh takes in writing on *Education and Political Power*. He shows clearly how the quality and quantity of provision for education depends on the power structure of society. If power is held by one, a dictator, there is one educational result. If it is held by a few, an elite, another result occurs. Of course, there is still a third result where the many, as in a democracy, are invested with power. There is hardly an area of education which is unaffected by the ramifications of this analysis.

JOHN S. BRUBACHER
Content Editor

Contents

CHAPTER I

Education and Political Theory   1

   Man: A Political Animal   2
   The Kinds of Political Systems   5
   Education: A State Function   8
   Education: Formal and Informal   9

CHAPTER II

Education and Rule by The One   10

   The Contemporary World Scene   10
   Attitudes Toward Education   11
   Purposes of Education   13
   Quantity and Quality of Education   14
   Direct Influences in the Classroom   17

CHAPTER III

Education and Rule by The Few   20

   The Contemporary World Scene   20
   Attitudes Toward Education   26
   Purpose of Education   28
   Quantity and Quality of Education   30
   Direct Influences in the Classroom   31

CHAPTER IV

Education and Rule by The Many 34

The Contemporary World Scene 35
Attitudes Toward Education 39
Purpose of Education 43
Quantity and Quality of Education 48
Direct Influences in the Classroom 50

CHAPTER V

Education and Growth toward Democracy 54

The Bases of Democracy 54
Democracy not Inevitable 58
Education Essential to the Establishing of Democracy 62
Education "About" and "In" Democracy 65
Education and Legislation 67

CHAPTER VI

Education Strengthened by Democracy 70

Dignity of the Individual 70
Equal Opportunity 73
Freedom of Inquiry 77
Self-Criticism and Evaluation 79
Creativity and Change 81

CHAPTER VII

Problems of Education in a Democracy 85

The Integrity of Education 85
Public and Private Education 87

The Financial Problem   91
Thought and Action   93

CHAPTER VIII

Education for the Future   99

Leadership and Public Service   101
Intercultural Education   103

Bibliography   107

Index   111

CHAPTER I

Education and Political Theory

Raw data for a study of this kind are neither as readily identifiable as the layman might like nor as exact and manageable as the educator might like. Nonetheless, the main thesis of this monograph is one with which both lay persons and educators would probably agree on first hearing. Perhaps the very fact that the thesis is seemingly commonplace helps to account for its not having been analyzed as fully as its importance would have merited. Most of the great philosophers have included treatises on education among their writings. There have been numerous excellent studies of the relationships between education and political rule in individual countries or systems. But it appears there has not been sufficient attention paid either to the underlying principles of this thesis or to its applications in anything akin to what the physical scientists call a "unified field theory."

Most succinctly the thesis is this: the status of education in any society or in any country is a direct correlative of the mode of political organization of that society or country. Another way of putting the thesis might be this: those in political control tend to see in the educational system a most effective means for furthering the objectives they espouse. If these objectives are valid and realistic, education will, other things being equal, prosper and thrive. If the objectives are invalid—i.e., if they are not genuinely in the individual and the public interest—then education will either be deliberately and drastically curtailed, or it will become a tool for advancing causes and cults or for perpetuating the power structure.

A unified theory would have to include, among other things, studies of the relationships between economic conditions and education, between sociological development and education, between levels of psychological sophistication and education, and even between climate or geographical location and education. Among all these, though, there are many senses in which the study of the relationship between modes of political organization and education are at once the primary and most fundamental ones. This study will be limited to them.

Man: A Political Animal

The analysis of the relationships between education and political systems begins with the fact that man is, as Aristotle pointed out, a political animal. The English words *politics* and *political* stem from the Greek word *polis* meaning *city*, and suggest the carrying out of the work and the life of the city. In this sense each man is a member of a polity, of a city, whatever form of organization that polity might take. What Aristotle meant to set forth, in defining man as a political animal,[1] is a fact based both on common observation and the dictates of reason. By himself man could survive, if at all, only with greatest difficulty and he could never advance himself. Even the most primitive men join together in rudimentary societies. And as soon as they come together in groups, an implicit or an explicit constitution emerges.

The framing of a formal constitution is a work of high intelligence, and it is one of the evident bases for the claim that man is essentially different from lower animals. Men are the only animals capable of governing themselves *constitutionally*. The constitution serves to inform each member of the group of what he may do and may not do. It informs him of the penalty attached to certain actions that endanger the common good but, more important, it informs him by whom and by what means important decisions regarding the welfare of the group are to be made.

If man is essentially a political animal, then it follows that Aristotle's further generalization that politics is the supreme practical art is correct.[2] Politics, in the broadest sense, is the way in which people live together and govern themselves for the mutual advantage of all and for the highest possible fulfillment of each. As such,

---

[1] "In this sense, Aristotle's statement that man is by nature a political animal holds with great exactitude: man is a political animal because he is a rational animal, because reason requires development through character training, education and the cooperation of other men, and because society is thus indispensable to the accomplishment of human dignity." Jacques Maritain, *The Person and The Common Good* (New York: Charles Scribner's Sons, 1947), pp. 38–39. Translated by John J. Fitzgerald.

[2] "The end of politics is the human good; it is the highest end in human things." St. Thomas, in *Ethics*, I, II. *Ibid.*, p. 19.

politics is an art rather than a science because it involves decisions based on prudence rather than on clear and certain knowledge. Politics has been called the art of the possible. It is not speculative, descriptive, or theoretical. It requires the best action in the light of all the circumstances. It is the supreme practical art both because it seeks to achieve the good of all and because it orders and directs the actions of men toward the achievement of this good. In this light, nothing could be further from the truth than the all-too-prevalent feeling in the modern world that politics is degrading or of little consequence. The more complex a society becomes, the more vital it is that politics be rightly understood and exercised.

Different groups organize themselves in different ways for the meeting of their needs and the achieving of their ends. As these differences become more structured and permanent, distinct political systems can be recognized. A group can be said to have a political system when its organization has reached a level at which there is both consistency among the parts and clear-cut differentiations within the functioning of the body politic. System entails a clear-cut assignment of rights and duties and of prerogatives and responsibilities. A political system is thus the whole complex of ways in which a group carries on the work of governing itself or of being governed.

Political systems not independent of historical conditions. There was a tendency among some earlier political theorists to assume that political systems which are objectively best or more appropriate—i.e., those which do in fact best contribute to the common good and to personal fulfillment—are therefore necessarily the best and most appropriate for all groups. This view is not held widely, if it is held at all, today. One of history's clearest lessons is that some political systems can work only when the people are sufficiently educated and sufficiently interested and responsible. A political system that might be appropriate for a people at one stage of its development may not be at all appropriate at another.

Perhaps the easiest way to establish that political systems are dependent upon certain historical conditions is to point out that when, for example, a people's main preoccupation is with the basic necessities of life—food, clothing, and shelter—a political system in which decisions are reached only after careful deliberation and the consent of a majority might be too slow and ineffective. Such a people might not be *economically* ready for, as an example, constitutional democracy. In a period of crisis or transition, rule by one man or by a small group of men might be necessary for survival.

From another, though related, point of view, people might not be *educationally* ready for democracy. An emerging country in which literacy is at a low level and in which education is neither sought nor valued cannot hope to govern itself democratically. If the people do not understand the issues and do not have sufficient knowledge on which to cast their vote, democracy is not only meaningless, it could also be dangerous.

Furthermore, at a given historical stage in its existence, a people might not be *psychologically* ready for democracy or emotionally disposed toward it. The mores or traditions of a given group might well incline that group to prefer to have its major political decisions made for it. For example, a nation with strong and deep-rooted convictions about the relationship between religious authority and secular power might well regard democratic self-government as a usurpation of divine jurisdiction. One thinks here, for example, of Old Testament theocracy, of pre-World War II Japan, and of modern Tibet.

Finally, a militaristic nation cannot be truly a democratic nation. Whether a nation adopts militarism to further its own purposes or ambitions or is forced to a militaristic posture in order to defend itself, it must curtail the flow of information and the degree of participation in decision-making necessary for a free and democratic society. As history shows, many nations and many groups have been militaristic, in attitude if not in fact, during the entire course of their existence.

The principal reason for pointing out that political systems are not actually independent of historical conditions is that any attempt to classify or categorize political systems necessarily prescinds from these individual conditions. Theoretical classification and analysis cannot take into account the many shades of difference which exist among individual political systems. Political systems are not static or stable. There is a constant movement within each system and among all systems to adapt themselves to changing conditions, demands, and pressures. For example, a weak democracy readily gives way to a strong dictatorship; a ruthless dictatorship is toppled and a military junta takes over; the rights of the people are ignored and the people rise in revolt to establish a constitutional democracy.

But some effort at classification, however inadequate, is necessary for clarifying the relationship between political systems and education.

The Kinds of Political Systems

For purposes of this study, the classification of political systems first found in Aristotle's *Politics* is most valuable. Though Aristotle is sometimes accused of placing too heavy an emphasis on deductive reasoning, it has long been established that his *Politics* was written only after the most intensive study of all the individual forms of political systems existing in his time. He states that political systems can best be distinguished on the basis of whether rule in them resides in *the one, the few,* or *the many*.

Rule is the all-inclusive word used by Aristotle to denote authority in any society. Authority is the organized physical and moral power of the state, and government is the formal agency for the exercising of political authority. Why are authority and government necessary for the well-being of both society and the individual?

Without authority, organization—the essential key to unity and continuity in society—is impossible. The more highly organized the society, the more necessary genuine authority becomes. Authority, properly exercised and limited, is the only safeguard against arbitrary, capricious, or chaotic action. If there were no authority, no rule, in society, there could be neither ordered activity nor recourse for injustice. The individual would be free to act in what he considered to be his own best interests, regardless of the legitimate and proper interest of others.

Throughout history there has been a stream of speculation as to what would result if there were no rule and no government other than the individual rule of good education and good conscience. Perhaps Rousseau most notably epitomizes this thought. Rousseau maintains that man is good by nature and that, unfettered by external rule, he would govern himself well and live in accord and concord with his fellow men. The speculation is not an idle one and even Yves Simon, in his excellent book, *The Philosophy of Democratic Government*, pays heed to it when he considers whether there would be any need for authority if men were both virtuous and wise.

Much more important than its negative role of safeguarding the rights of both man and society is the positive purpose and function of authority: the advancement and promotion of the common good. Authority sets forth the principles and procedures by which order and reason are introduced into the relationships and actions within and among individuals and groups. It provides the framework within which laws are enacted and executed and conflicts of rights and responsibilities are adjudicated. Authority binds people together in common pursuit of the general welfare. It provides for orderly, rather than violent, changes in the society and it both symbolizes and makes possible the striving of all persons for the good life in a world in which all things are limited and in which all persons are imperfect.

Rule, then, government or authority, is the basis for Aristotle's distinction of political systems into those in which *the one* rules, *the few* rule, or *the many* rule. There is no political system that does not fall into one or another of these categories.

Rule by *the one* implies that all authority over a group and all government of that group reside ultimately in one person. Whether he derives his authority from the consent of those governed, from military power, from God (e.g., the Divine Right of kings), or from an established primogeniture, all power—including that over life and death—belongs to him.

As is true of all other systems of political organizations, rule by *the one* can be either in the public interest or contrary to the public interest. If it is in the public interest, it is called *monarchy* (which means literally *rule by one*). When it is in the public interest, rule by *the one* is sometimes called *benevolent despotism*. If it is contrary to the public interest or the common good, it is traditionally called *tyranny* or, in more modern times, *dictatorship*. The tyrant or dictator rules out of personal or selfish motives or for some personal gain and he is called a tyrant or dictator to the extent that he neglects the welfare of those over whom he has authority. It is entirely possible, of course, that a tyrant or dictator will succeed in deluding himself into believing he rules in the public interest, and he will, if necessary, take steps to convince the people of this.

Rule by *the few* suggests that some particular group exercises rule or authority in a given society. This form of political organization is called *aristocracy* (*rule by the best*) if the group rules in the public interest. It is called *oligarchy* (*rule by the few*) if the group rules contrary to the public interest. Rule by *the few* may take a number of different forms. Many primitive tribes were ruled by a group of council members. Often council members were selected because of their success in the hunt or on the field of battle. In Europe the governing groups were composed of nobles selected by reason of their birth, their wealth, or (less commonly) their intelligence. Today, in Communist countries, the ruling group is composed of Communist Party members.

The phrase *rule by the many* might be somewhat misleading. It really means *rule by all*. It implies that ultimate authority belongs to all persons and equally to each person. It is called *democracy* if it is rule in the public interest and *mobocracy* if it is not. The term *rule by the many* is not at all synonomous with the term *rule by the majority*. *Rule by the many* or *rule by all* indicates the ultimate source and repository of authority. *Rule by the majority* is a convenient operational concept—a way of reaching agreement when unanimity is impossible. The theory is that if more of the people are for an action than are opposed to it, that action has the best chance of being the right one. In a democracy, the minority always keeps its right to vote. It also keeps its right to rule, if and when it wins enough persons to its side to become a majority.

Rule by the many does not imply that every member of the group actually engages in the process of ruling—although in some small groups (such as the New England communities of the seventeenth and eighteenth centuries) this is not impossible. *Rule by the many* ordinarily means that governing power or authority is delegated by the group to certain persons who exercise this power with the consent, and in accordance with the wishes, of those whom they represent. *Rule by the many* also implies orderly processes and informed and responsible leaders whose function it is to promote the general welfare.

What is called *mobocracy* is really not rule by *the many* but rule by a frenzied few whom *the many*—or the mob—follow unthinkingly. It is rule by emotion and without restraint and, since it implies the breakdown of law and order, it is not, of course, in the public interest. Mobocracy has been the form of rule in certain countries at certain times when needed reform could not be brought about by lawful processes and when, in the absence of good leadership, the people rose as a mob in violent revolution.

Aristotle's tripartite classification of rule or governments is intended to have the broadest possible scope. It includes, but is not limited to, the rule or the government of a State. It extends to rule in every and any form of human association; for example, the family, the Church, the school or university, and even to business and industry. It is quite clear, further, that Aristotle's classification of the forms of rule is not at all limited to the external framework of governments. It does, in fact, refer to the determinants of power and to the actual conduct of rule and authority within groups, including the government of the State. Aristotle's classification has precisely the great advantage that it simplifies the study of both the external frameworks of governments and the vital moving forces of social power. Power, both in name and in fact, resides with *the one, the few,* or *the many* in every form of human organization.

Education: A State Function

The principle that education is a primary and major function of the State has long been taken for granted in advanced countries and cultures and it is rapidly coming to be taken for granted in those areas of the world said to be emerging or developing. An understanding of the principle that education is rightly a function of the State is essential to any study of the relationship between education and political systems.

First of all, to say that education is a primary concern and major function of the State is not to say that the State is either the primary or major agency of education. Both the family and the Church have antecedent educational rights and responsibilities. But in its own best interests and because of its unique position, the State—however constituted—should not and cannot neglect its role in the education of all persons of all age groups.

No matter how primitive or how advanced, each State depends for its preservation and progress on a widespread understanding and sharing of fundamental life-concepts and life-values. The people of that State must be able to communicate, to interpret experiences, to detect regularities and laws, to discern the real from the illusory, and to differentiate the good from the evil. Of course, these concepts and values will be more or less sophisticated depending on the level of advancement of the society, but they will all be based on learning. No man comes to any level of knowledge simply through his own discovery. If the State is to survive at all, if it is to make any progress, and if it is to fulfill its essential role for existing, namely to promote the common welfare, then it must see to it that each citizen receives, through whatever means, an education sufficient to make him an effective member of society. Among its many responsibilities in promoting the common welfare, there is none more basic to the State than the promotion of education. The State's regard for individual human dignity as well as the precepts of social welfare and social justice require it to fulfill this responsibility.

Furthermore, the State is ordinarily the only agency which has the regulatory or the coercive power and the financial means to make sure that education is carried on and pursued. The State may make whatever arrangements for education it deems most appropriate, but it cannot abrogate its basic responsibility in this matter.

Education: Formal and Informal

A final and elementary distinction must be introduced here: the educative process can be either formal or informal. All education, except that which is strictly the act of discovery—and this is very limited—requires the assistance of another, of a teacher. Education is said to be formal when learning is systematic and programmed. The school is the agency of formal education, and a school, in this sense, can be of any size and of any organizational pattern. Education is said to be informal when learning comes about as the result of daily life experiences. Such education as one might receive from the mass communication media, the society's legislative enactments and judicial decisions, and the ordinary course of conversation with one's fellows would be examples of informal education.

It will be evident, through this distinction, that the schools are by no means the only sources of education. Some may even question whether they are the most effective sources, contending that education in "real-life" situations is always more effective than that in artificial school environments. Although the subsequent analysis will deal with formal education, there is at all times close correlation, as well, between the modes of political organization and the informal sources or means of education.

CHAPTER II

Education and Rule by The One

Rule by *the one* is by no means a thing of the past. Neither is it, as some political theorists maintain, necessarily a matter of time until the last vestiges of rule by *the one* will have disappeared under the rising tide of popular demand for democracy. Rule by *the one*, rightly or wrongly, answers a twofold tendency in human history and human nature and there will most likely always be a strong impulse toward it.

On the one hand, rule by *the one* epitomizes authority. It represents decisiveness and efficiency. It offers a single living symbol of unity. It supplies the people a specific hero when things are going well and a scapegoat when things go badly. On the other hand, it is the culmination of power and, consequently, a prized goal for men who seek such power. Man's drive toward power can not be dismissed lightly. To attain sole and uncontestable power over a country or a society is, for some men, an ambition worthy of their best and worst efforts.

The Contemporary World Scene

It would be impossible, of course, to examine in detail the systems of political organization in each of the countries of the world in which rule by *the one* prevails. Nor would it be to the point to attempt to pass judgment on whether such governments are currently serving the public interest. The fact is, however, that many such forms of government—in name or in fact—do exist and do exercise great influence over the lives of their own and other peoples.

Monarchies. There are several monarchies in the modern world, to be sure, but a number of these are monarchies in name only. The power of such monarchies is limited by written or unwritten constitutions. Their main function is a traditional or ceremonial one, although in some cases the monarch retains a high degree of power in appointing government officers and approving legislation.

10

In many of the less-developed countries, rule by *the one* resides either with a king or with a tribal chief. In these cases, the monarch has almost unlimited power. His word is still the law; his authority final and absolute.

Dictatorships. The twentieth century has seen a rapid expansion of rule by *the one* in the form of the modern dictatorship. It has been estimated that this century has already given rise to as many dictatorships as it has democracies. The dictator seizes power and maintains it by liquidating or imprisoning his personal or political enemies. Whatever his motivations, the dictator rules with monolithic and unilateral authority. His decision is law not because he represents the will of the people but because he has the force to make it law.

Finally, monarchies and dictatorships are both forms of rule by *the one*. They are similar in this respect, although they may be vastly different in many important ways. For this study, the main point to consider is that, inevitably and in a manner clearly traceable, government by *the one* leads to certain patterns of educational thinking and procedure. There will be exceptions to every generalization and no generalization applies with equal validity to all cases; nonetheless, the patterns are quite clear.

Attitudes Toward Education

What is the typical attitude toward education of those countries in which rule is by *the one?*

From the political point of view, where rule by *the one* obtains it is thought to be relatively unimportant for citizens to be informed and thus capable of making their own decisions. All the major decisions, including those most directly affecting the life of the individual and the country, are made by *the one*. Indeed, education is thought to be diversionary and deviationist to the extent that it interferes with or impedes the full implementation of the ruler's policies and programs. The natural inclination of either the monarch or dictator is to desire to remain in power. He has no established term of office and his remaining in office depends either on firm adherence by the populace to the basic prerogative which put him in office or on his careful control of any ideas or any forces which might unseat him.

Education in itself is regarded as a force leading to change and for that reason attitudes toward it are cautious and restrictive. Any ideas that appear threatening or dangerous cannot be tolerated in a situation in which the ruling power sees himself as the interpreter of the way of life and the planner of the ways of thinking and acting of the persons he rules. His position is weakened to the extent that doubts are allowed to creep in, and open education inevitably leads to independent judgment, sharp analysis, questioning, and doubt. In those cases in which rule is by *the one,* the ruler must keep his subjects subservient and dependent. He does not think of education as an ally in this effort.

Therefore, neither the monarch nor the dictator has traditionally been a friend of education. History reveals that few monarchs have made the advancing of education one of their primary concerns. There have been some: Charlemagne, for example, and certain of the later German princes. Henry VIII is said to have taken an active interest in the University early in his reign. Japan, under its emperors, had a good but limited system of education. An occasional altruistic and enlightened monarch, wishing the best for his people, will allow certain types of education to flourish as a means of uplifting and strengthening his nation. Ordinarily, however, even this takes the form of permitting education to develop rather than that of taking the leadership in promoting it.

The monarch or dictator may have had ample schooling but he is rarely, if ever, a well-educated man himself. In the case of the monarch, his education will have been carefully planned and he will have been exposed only to the "right" ideas. The man who rules alone is ordinarily a man of action and a man of firm but unreasoned convictions. Those who have not personally experienced both the delights and the practical value of education are not likely to hold it in high esteem. Other projects will take precedence in the allocation of available funds, teachers will be hard to find and will be held in low repute, teaching will be doctrinaire and insipid, and educational facilities will be minimal. Constant surveillance will be exercised and education will be harnessed to preserve accepted modes of life and thought.

Purposes of Education

Yet education is so much a part of life at all times and so much a necessity in the modern world that no monarch or dictator could suppress it altogether, even if he should so desire. Formal education is an established fact in every country in the world, although in many parts it is still rudimentary and, in the term popularized by UNESCO, "basic." Roughly half of the world's population can neither read nor write.

Education in those countries ruled by one person tends to be directed primarily and almost exclusively to the service of the State. It is an instrument of national policy. Its ends are most likely to be technological, developmental, and even military. Education is valued as a means of increasing the State's ability to survive and to compete in the power struggle from which no State is immune. Education is also employed as a means of attaining unity and some degree of concerted action. Without some education it is impossible to shoot a gun or to drive a tractor. It is impossible to follow orders unless one can understand the words in which it is given. It is to the advantage of the State and the ruler to have a literate citizenry.

But the main purpose of education in a monarchy or dictatorship is ideological. All education is geared to preserving and strengthening the ideology and to deepening its acceptance rather than to analyzing or criticizing it. At the same time the educational system seeks to produce scientists and technologists, it seeks to hold rigidly to its fundamental ideology. No phase of the system escapes this overriding purpose and that purpose is always pre-established and held to be both superior and ulterior to the purposes of the individual himself. Indeed, the individual never gets the opportunity to determine for himself what the intrinsic purpose of education might be. The criterion for establishing the value of education is whether it advances the cause outlined by the monarch or dictator. If it veers from this course, it may be forcibly brought back into line.

Inevitably, education in a monarchy or a dictatorship gives rise to, and capitalizes on, the cult of the personality of the leader. Since the basic answer to certain fundamental questions must always be "because King X or Dictator Y says so," the ruler is invested with powers and prerogatives that center simply on his own being and his own person. His image is glorified in pictures and statues. His

achievements are magnified, if not manufactured. His pronouncements become oracular. He is the final arbiter of truth. The educational system seeks to convince youngsters and adults alike that the
leader knows what is best and that they can do no better than to
follow him. The cult of personality is, like all cults, emotional. It
can be powerful and persuasive, but it is hardly an adequate substitute for education.

A final clearly recognized purpose of education in most monarchies or dictatorships is the production of a class of people who
can carry on the work proper to the professions. Law, medicine,
engineering, architecture are pursued in order to keep the people
reasonably happy and convinced that progress is being made. Ordinarily, such professional studies are not considered a threat to the
regime but, rather, a support for it.

Quantity and Quality of Education

The fact that a country or society is organized in such a way that
political rule and power is controlled by one man has unavoidable
implications for both the quantity and the quality of education made
available.

When the *quantity* of education is considered, there are two
factors: the amount of education available and the number of students to whom it is available. There is a small or a large quantity
of education available depending on how much there is for how
many. For example, as of now for all practical purposes a high
school education is available, and even compulsory, to all American
youngsters, whether boy or girl, and whether Caucasian, Negro, or
Asian, whether Catholic, Protestant, Jew, or atheist. This quantity
of education would not have been available even fifty years ago.

When the *quality* of education is analyzed the concern is with
the educative effort itself and with its impact. Is the education
offered good education? Are the teachers fully qualified? Are the
students encouraged and challenged? Does the education meet the
needs of the students? Are the necessary facilities and the necessary
equipment on hand? Does the society itself put a high value on education so that the efforts of the schools are constantly reinforced
by the parents, by the Church, by peer groups, and by the other
institutions in society?

When the rule or power of a country is centered in one man, the quantity of education available tends to be minimal. This generalization, of course, must be modified according to the stage of development of the country under consideration and the purposes and plans and the degree of enlightenment of the ruler. But it is generally true. The ruler thinks of education as an intrusion rather than as an investment. The people grow accustomed to a life without education. Money that might be put into education will be used for other purposes. Even when, for example, through such relatively inexpensive means as educational radio and television, education could be made generally available, the ruler tends to resist it and to withhold financing from it. Few people will be educated to any degree at all and practically none will have the advantage of pursuing advanced studies.

The ideas of universal education and compulsory education are, of course, relatively recent ideas in every land. But in a country ruled by one, many of the children can never expect to receive more than a rudimentary education. Those who are to be educated, a small percentage of the educable youth, will ordinarily come from the more influential and fully indoctrinated groups. They will be sent to the schools held to be reliable and established and maintained for the purposes proper to the State. They will remain in school only as long as the State or the ruler decrees. But there is no inner logic or dynamic in such a society which might give to education an upward and outward thrust. Those who finish elementary education will feel no strong motivation to continue into secondary school and college, even if these schools should be available to them.

Viewed from the qualitative point of view, therefore, even that quantity of education which is available in a society ruled by *the one* is most likely to be uninspired. It is likely to be closely supervised, highly standardized, and carefully controlled. It will be neither open nor creative education. The emphasis will be more on filling the mind of the students with safe and accepted ideas rather than on urging them to explore new ideas and to think them through for themselves.

Whether the form of government is monarchial or dictatorial, it tends to be conservative and traditional. The monarch's power depends on his preserving the tradition that brought him to power. Dictators often come into power as the result of a revolution, but once in power their first course of action is to prevent—by force if necessary—any counterrevolutionary thinking or activity. Their tradition may not be as deeply rooted as that of the monarch but it is every bit as binding. J. Ortega y Gasset describes the quality of education in a traditional and conservative society:

> So long as the empire of tradition lasts, each unit of mankind remains imbedded in the close corporation of communal existence. He does nothing on his own account, apart from the social group. He is not the protagonist of his own acts. His personality is not his own, distinct from others; an identical mind is reproduced in each unit with the same thoughts, memories, desires, and emotions. Hence, in traditionalist centuries figures of outstanding personal physiognomy are not, as a rule, to be found. All the members of the social body are more or less the same. The only important differences are those of position, rank, employment or class. . . .[1]

The quality of education in a country ruled by *the one* is inevitably determined by the desire of the ruler to maintain the traditions of that country and reinforce its underlying ideas and modes of thought. The result is a kind of cycle. The teachers of the upcoming generation are those who have demonstrated their agreement with the traditional ideas. Even teacher-preparation programs are so designed as to make sure that the future teachers do not embark on new programs or search too deeply into ideas that are likely to be dangerous or disturbing. When they become teachers, these persons, naturally enough, follow the same ideas and procedures which they have learned are safe and satisfactory. In turn, their students will be those who most docilely accept the traditional patterns of thought. The teacher's encomiums go, too, to those students who seek new ways of verifying or illustrating the traditional ideas and making them his own, not to those who seek to look outside the system.

Education in this context is ordinarily of low quality because it is more concerned with the past than with the future. It guards too closely the "given" ideas and it tends to place a premium on conformity and passivity. Since it is handed down, it tends to be informational rather than exploratory. There is little opportunity to exercise individual and independent judgment and there is little of

---

[1] J. Ortega y Gasset, *The Modern Theme* (New York: W. W. Norton & Co., 1922). Quoted in the *Nature of Politics*, edited by Michael Curtis (New York: Avon Book Division of The Hearst Corporation, 1962), p. 62.

the stimulation that results from the clash of divergent opinions and possibilities. Such education continually runs the risk of becoming unmindful of, or irrelevant to, its own time, rather than shaping it and, through it, the future.

Direct Influences in the Classroom

Finally, it remains to examine what direct influence rule by *the one* has in the classroom. The first and most obvious influence is in the classroom concept itself and in its nature and organization. The classroom with its thirty, forty, or more students sitting in fixed seats and facing a teacher may perhaps be explained on the grounds of administrative economy and efficiency. But it also reflects the influence of a theory of education in which learning and ideas are previously and neatly arranged for distribution to the students. This type of classroom serves well the educational needs of a society in which all decisions are made by one person.

The curriculum. The basic meaning of *curriculum* is the program or course of studies to be followed by the student. That there is such a thing as a curriculum implies that someone has selected, from the vast range of knowledge, those ideas which merit special attention.

In a country ruled by *the one,* the curriculum at all levels of formal education will tend to be rigidly organized and structured. There will be close control over what is to be studied and read and there will be clear-cut prohibitions against certain books and ideas. The curriculum will be planned for the student on the principle that those in charge know what is best and most appropriate for him. The curriculum will embody and highlight those ideas which he is expected to accept—those of which the ruler approves or which present no conflict with the approved doctrine.

Political rule by *the one* directly influences the curriculum in the classroom in that it tends to place emphasis on those subjects which lead to the most immediate and practical results and which are most neutral from the human point of view. By occupying the student in these pursuits, the regime will thus be able to make scientific and technological progress without running the risk of opening up ideological controversy. Concentration on science and technology permits progress and a build-up of prestige and it helps to close the mind to those fundamental theological and philosophical questions in which the regime is most vulnerable. Since science and technology play a supportive role to the political regime, the best minds, the best teachers and research personnel, and the best students are drawn into these fields. There they find the least danger, the largest financial rewards, and the most recognition by the political authority.

The humanities and the fine arts suffer in the curriculum both by default and because they are officially regarded as of little worth. Their deepest and most genuine purpose is not appreciated and their spirit is suspected. Literature is studied only to the extent that it is politically useful. The study of foreign languages is a large part of the curriculum both because of its pragmatic value and its nonideological character.

Social studies, if they are pursued at all, are narrowly circumscribed or warped to meet the demands of the ruling force. For example, history becomes a kind of mythology in an attempt to further nationalistic goals and as an instrument for justifying the right to rule of the monarch or the dictator. Sociology cannot be objective because it might bring to light conditions which would be best, in the interests of the ruling power, left unexamined. Civics and political science become a glorification of present forms rather than either a comparative or an analytic study of possible systems.

Methods of teaching. Teaching methods themselves tend directly to parallel forms of political organization. Where political authority resides in *the one,* the teacher will—perhaps even unconsciously—adopt teaching methods and techniques similar to the methods of rule prevailing in political life. He tends to demand from his students the same kinds of discipline, respect, and conformity which he encounters in his own life outside the classroom. This is the only way of ruling he knows and his classroom is his domain, his chance to rule. His students, too, become very willing to look on the teacher as a symbol or substitute for the type of authority which prevails in the society as a whole.

The teacher's approach to his teaching and to his various subject matters will be one of tight organization. Just as in society at large, everything will be expected to fall neatly into place. Ordinarily his teaching methods will be much more logical than psychological. He has a certain amount of material to "cover" in a prescribed amount of time and he knows exactly how he intends to cover it. Consequently, too, the instruction will be largely verbal rather than experiential. The teacher, of course, is likely to think of his profession as one filled with routine and leaving very little to his own judgment because his instruction will be highly standardized and impersonal. Rule by *the one* leads to fixed patterns and fixed objectives. Teaching and learning both become matters of regimentation and not of exciting quest or conquest.

In a country ruled by *the one,* all teaching methods will be aimed at getting the "right" results, which will have been predetermined. The teacher will seek to motivate the student by rewarding him for coming to the "right" conclusions and for thinking along the "right" lines. The teacher will realize his responsibility for securing the "right" results from his students. He is likely to be convincing and at times even inspiring. His positions will be bold and clear-cut and the student will experience the value of contact with a forceful, though closed, mind.

CHAPTER III

Education and Rule by The Few

Rule by *the few* is a form of government or rule that stands, in a sense, midway between rule by *the one* and rule by *the many*. On the one hand, it seeks to avoid the arbitrariness and absoluteness associated with bestowing final power on any one man. On the other, it maintains that rule by *the many* might lead to rule by people who are incompetent, uninformed, highly emotional, and irresponsible. Rule by *the few* is based on the principle that in any group, country, or society there are some who are best qualified to rule or govern and that power should be given to them.

Rule by *the few* will show in its relationships to education some of the characteristics of rule by *the one* and some of rule by *the many*. It will also have distinctive correlations of its own. On the whole, however, education will be more closely allied, both in theory and in practice, to that found in countries ruled by *the one* than it is to that in countries ruled by *the many*.

The Contemporary World Scene

What does *rule by the few* mean in the modern world and what, and where, are the examples of it? An example or two taken from the nonpolitical world will serve as a good illustration of the theory of rule by the few.

In many large American business corporations, final decisions of policy rest with a board of directors. No one individual alone, not even the chairman of the board, makes the important corporate decisions. The corporation makes no pretense of extending the right to vote on ordinary operational matters to all persons having a share in the business. In this sense, the board members are the "aristocracy" of the corporation. However, the board of directors is responsible, in turn, to all the stockholders of the corporation, and the directors may be removed by vote of the stockholders.

Another example is found in many universities in which a board of trustees is the final decision-making body. Neither the faculty nor the student body, although they are vitally involved in the work of the university and are deeply concerned with its welfare, has a vote in the matters falling under the jurisdiction of the board.

In political affairs, rule by *the few* is very much a part of the present world scene. It is not the purpose of this monograph to attempt to pass judgment on whether a particular regime is or is not in the public interest. Each will claim to be and each, depending on circumstances far beyond the range of this monograph, may or may not be. For that reason, reference will be made only to aristocracies rather than to both aristocracies and oligarchies.

An aristocratic arrangement has several advantages. It makes provision for the consideration of different points of view before a final action is taken. It also provides for an inner system of checks and balances so that no one person can arrogate dictatorial power to himself. It permits relative speed and efficiency. At the same time it must rely for its continued existence, in the midst of pressure from both internal and external dissenting voices, on leadership and persuasion rather than on the use of force alone.

It also has several disadvantages. It gives rise to an almost constant power struggle within the aristocratic group itself. It tends to set off the elite or ruling group from those who are ruled. The danger is that the elite group will come to think that its best interests represent the best interests of all the people. It makes difficult the kind of secrecy which is sometimes necessary when a new idea is being explored or a change is contemplated. It leaves unresolved the question of where the power actually resides, in those frequent cases in which the ruling group itself is evenly divided on an action to be taken. In a close decision, the power may actually reside in the vote or voice of a single person. In discussing the nature of rule by the few, Simon points out:

> Experience shows that the operation of elites is not reassuring for those who happen not to be included in any recognized elite. Even if it were possible to designate infallibly, through a process which would have to be magical, men perfectly qualified for government, it would still be a good precaution to erect, in front of such a chosen few, as a check and complement, the power of numbers. An elite, even if it were supposed to be genuine, can hardly escape the

all-too-human temptation to think in terms of the elite and to ignore the problems of the many.[1]

The contemporary world scene offers several examples of how modern rule by *the few* is effectively carried on. It also presents examples of the various grounds on which ruling groups or elites come into power.

Aristocracy of blood. Probably the oldest and most commonly understood type of aristocracy is that of blood. It implies that those who are related in some line of consanguinity with the father or founder of the ruling line retain the right to rule by reason of this relationship. This formal aristocracy is enlarged through intermarriage and in some cases is granted to those outside the actual blood line as reward for exceptionally meritorious service or action. Aristocrats of the blood fall into several different kinds of groupings and categories, each with clear-cut titles and each with specific functions. The concept of an aristocracy of blood has carried over even to the relation between races, with certain persons of one race regarding themselves as superior to the members of other races. But in all cases it is the aristocrats, collectively, who control the power. No one individual can rule independently or in his own name.

In those countries where an aristocracy of blood holds the power, there is likely to be an almost continuous struggle, latent or overt, between the nobles and the highest single executive authority. The king, for example, considers that final power resides with him, but the lords prefer to think of the king as a *primus inter pares,* simply *the first among equals.* History, however, points to a common tendency for the nobles and the monarch to form a coalition against any demands for power made by the masses.

Aristocracy of wealth. Throughout history there has been a close connection between aristocracy and the possession and control of wealth. The aristocratic groups have usually been the wealthy or the privileged groups. The asistocrats were the propertied people and the landholders. Until fairly recently, however, the right to power and the exercise of power continued to be based on blood rather than wealth. Wealth was a concommitant of power, but not a reason for it.

Modern history, however, has introduced a new kind of aristoc-

---

[1] Yves R. Simon, *Philosophy of Democratic Government* (Chicago: University of Chicago Press, 1951), p. 98.

racy—that which rules by reason of its wealth. The Industrial Age has brought immense wealth to those persons who have been able to capitalize on invention, discovery, and trade. With the accumulation and centralization of wealth has come power, not only in the marketplace but also in political spheres. Those in possession of wealth tend to band together to form an aristocracy which can readily convert its wishes and demands into political power. If the wealthy do not themselves seek political office, they are eager to make sure that only those who hold theoretical positions similar to their own do become the governing officials. In many countries, it requires wealth even to run for political office.

Aristocracy of military might.   Rule by *the few* is exercised in some countries in the modern world through an aristocracy of military might. Those who control the military resources of the country simply seize political power and retain it by exercise of sheer brute force. The actual power will customarily reside in a clique made up of the leaders of the army, the navy, and the police forces. In the absence of any higher civilian authority, the military junta becomes the established and ruling government. The soldiers, who are accustomed to taking orders from this group of men, now become the effective means of carrying out political rule.

The danger of a military coup has been a constant one in all stages of history. Military heroes are both popular and forceful. The army is a well-disciplined unit, trained to react promptly and without question to whatever orders are given it. Consequently, if for any reason there should be a falling out between civilian authorities and military leaders, the military have all the physical power of men and equipment at their command. The civilian authorities have none. It is a relatively easy matter for the military to take over quickly and completely.

At certain stages of historical development, the people of a country might possibly need the enforced discipline and the security which a military aristocracy affords them. Military might usually leads, at least, to some kind of order and organization. The people know what to expect. But it is usually misleading to think of military rule as temporary or transitional. Once established, the military aristocracy desires to retain power and it has the means necessary to do so. It can be dislodged only by a superior military force.

Aristocracy of intelligence.   The concept of an aristocracy of intelligence is one which finds advocates and spokesmen throughout practically all ages of history, but which rarely, if ever, finds actual historical embodiment. In its political sense, it means that rule should be in the hands of those persons who have the greatest intelligence and ability rather than in the hands of those who have military power or wealth or certain blood connections. In this view, man's best hope lies with those who have developed their rational powers to the fullest possible extent. The Utopians have consistently urged this mode of political organization.

Perhaps no one has put the matter more clearly or more forthrightly than Plato in *The Republic*. He advocated that the philosopher should be king in his plan for the ideal political order. The philosopher-king would rule well because he would know what good rule means and in what it consists. Plato's concept was more monarchical than aristocratic, but it gave philosophical legitimacy to a long line of educational theorists who maintained that one of education's principal tasks was to prepare an elite whose privilege and responsibility it would be to rule and to lead. Plato's thinking is still evident in the modern world. Many countries maintain schools which emphasize education for leadership. Candidates for these schools must meet high admissions standards which are based primarily on academic and intellectual achievement. Graduates of these schools form the aristocracy of intelligence and, it is hoped, are the leaders and rulers of the future.[2]

Aristocracy and ideology. Another important type of aristocracy has arisen in the modern world. This is the aristocracy of *the party*. The party is an organization of relatively few members firmly and fully committed to a particular ideology.

The most notable example is the Communist Party. Russia and China are the two best and largest examples of how this type of rule by *the few* works in the modern world. Earlier clear-cut examples of party rule would have been Nazi Germany and Fascist Italy. The actual number of members of the party is often very small in comparison with the number of people whom the party dominates. Only a few people make the decisions either about the basic party

---

[2] "Across the street from the Sorbonne in Paris, Louis-le-grand has an ancient passion to create 'an elite of the elite' and a modern penchant for vaulting brainy boy into the grandes ecoles, the suprauniversities whose graduates virtually run France." *Time* (May 17, 1963), 103

theories and principles or about how the party is to relate itself to
the nonparty public in the conduct of daily business. But the party
makes the decisions not only for its own party members but also for
all the people whom the party controls.[3]

The number of Communist Party members in Soviet Russia is
said to be less than 2 per cent of the entire population, and within
the Party itself all the important decisions are made by a small group
of men. Very often, in fact, the final decisions are made by one man,
the Party Secretary, although the decision is generally purported to
be the decision of the Presidium.

In connection with decision-making by the Party, Richard Hughes
writes:

> Despite all its faults and errors, the Communist regime has im-
> posed the first strong central government over a unified China in a
> hundred turbulent years of unleashed nationalism.
>
> There is still no written legal code in the country: law is laid
> down by empirical party decree. But the authority of the cadres and
> the pressure of organized Maoist persuasion compels at least passive
> mass loyalty. Only those writers who have never visited "liberated"
> China talk loosely of "a police state." To the sensitive Western
> liberal, the implications of Mao's "brute reason" may well be more
> horrifying than Stalin's "brute force," but at least physical terror
> is not the basis of Communism in China. The authority of the
> Central Government can be expected to be the more durable for
> that reason.[4]

Whatever the number comprising the new party aristocracy, the
important fact is that it is given over completely to an established
ideology. The party has a set of fixed and absolute principles to the
implementation of which the party is dedicated with a kind of mili-
tant zeal. Lines of development and courses of action are set in
advance in keeping with the ideological doctrine and there is no
compromise or deviation. The ideology is imposed by persuasion
if possible, but by force if necessary.

An ideology is the exact opposite of a liberal point of view or an
inquiring state of mind. It is anti-intellectualistic in the sense that

---

[3] "We also read in *Pravda* that 'the new man is not made by himself; it is the
Party which directs the whole process of the socialist re-creation and re-education
of the masses.'" Jacques Maritain, *True Humanism*, 6th ed. (New York: Charles
Scribner's Sons, 1954), p. 83. Translated by M. R. Adamson.

[4] Richard Hughes, "The 'Great Leap' is now the 'Great Retreat,' " *The New
York Times Magazine* (October 7, 1962), 86.

it is prescribed and allows no room for discussion or dissent. The more effective the hold of the ideology on the minds of its adherents, the more comprehensive and all-embracing are its effects. It extends to all phases of life and answers all questions in the light of preconceived ideas. For example, the official philosophical position of the Communist Party in modern Russia is one of dialectical materialism. This basic doctrine, as an interpretation of history, gives rise to a whole series of important derived principles which reach into every aspect of human life. One illustration: the official position of the Communist Party is atheistic. The question is no longer open and at least officially Party members must profess atheism. The individual has no choice. Communism, thus, is not simply an economic or a social theory; it is a total philosophy of life to which the Party member surrenders himself.

The aristocracy—in this case either the party or the party leaders —seeks to impose its ideology on everyone. The party is active and aggressive. When propagandizing and indoctrination fail, physical violence and force become the means for spreading the ideology. But it is not power exerted in any unplanned or short-range way; it is power aimed at establishing or preserving a new order in society based on a predesigned ideology and at eliminating or rendering ineffective those who are opposed to the ideology. Unlike the older aristocracies, in theory and often in practice, the party aristocracy does not seek riches or personal aggrandizement. Rather, it justifies its grasping of power by its dedication to the public good, to widespread social improvement, and to the bettering of economic conditions for all.

Attitudes Toward Education

The correlation between modes of political organization and patterns of education are nowhere more evident than in a country or society in which rule is by *the few*. In such countries education will most likely be regarded as *for the few*. It will be highly selective and highly competitive. Although widespread literacy is fostered, higher and advanced education will be open only to a small minority of the citizens. Large amounts of money will be spent for the education of the elite and only relatively small amounts for education of the masses. Education will tend to be static rather than dynamic and experimental. Acceptance of ideas rather than criticism of them will ordinarily be the motif of education.

Education for the few.   In a society in which a sharp distinction is made between *the few* and *the many* as a fundamental assumption of social organization, education almost inevitably makes the same distinction. It will be held that the few have need for types of knowledges and experiences that would be unnecessary or even harmful for the many. The contention—perhaps more covert than overt—is that in any society there are only a few persons who have sufficient ability and aptitude to benefit fully from a complete education. Whether or not this is a rationalization for the system, those who defend it claim that only these few are educable.

The correlative of this point of view is, of course, that in any society there are only a relatively few high-level positions. These must be filled by the real leaders in society. Even a successful and prosperous society has need for only a few well-educated persons. If a higher percentage of people are educated than the society can place or absorb, then the society will become overintellectualized, discontented, frustrated, and disaffected.

Education in such a society becomes highly competitive. Not only is it open only to a few on a selective and often discriminatory basis, but the very process of education is shot through with competitive overtones. Advancement in society is open only to the educated and the opportunity for further education is based on the achieving of marks and grades superior to those of one's classmates. Education becomes both a fierce conflict and a powerful weapon.[5]

Financing education.   In those countries ruled by *the few,* a much larger proportion of the education budget will go into the education of those privileged few who have been selected—on whatever basis—to get a full education than into the education of the masses. Although it is customarily thought to be important that literacy be widespread and that consumer interest be fairly sophisticated, there is a frank recognition that money should be spent where it will do the most good. Education of the leaders is more important to society than education of the followers and consequently those who are to

---

[5] Even in America where rule is by the many, the sociologists are quite generally agreed that the basic social differentiation is based on college degree. For example, those with college degrees tend to marry college graduates and to associate both in business and in social life only with those who have degrees.

be the leaders get the largest share of the education budget. Similarly, the portion of the total budget assigned to educational purposes will be relatively small compared to the portions assigned to other purposes. In some countries, training in the arts, skills, crafts, and trades will be provided for those who do not qualify for the more rigidly academic types of education.

Purpose of Education

Education in a society ruled by *the few* tends to take place within a closed system. Education is not regarded as a means of social mobility; it is an adjunct to a way of life largely determined by other conditions and choices. Education is not daring or experimental so much as it is a matter of seeking to understand the justification and interpretation of the prevailing ideology. Whatever serves this cause or purpose is regarded as "good" education. The aim of the schools at all levels is to strengthen the power which the ideology has over the minds and lives of those who fall under its domination. Thus education is really an instrument in the hands of the ruling body. This type of so-called education might better be labeled *indoctrination* or *orientation*, but it exerts a profound influence on those subjected to it.[6] It is calculated to serve the purposes of those who control it rather than the purposes of those who should be the primary concern of all education: the students.

To understand the purpose of education in a country ruled by *the few* and dominated by a particular ideology, it is necessary to understand the way in which that ideology regards the individual person or citizen. Generally, at least in modern times, the ideology relates the person to some concept or cause—perhaps race or class —to which the person is inferior and subordinate. The individual is regarded as important only to the extent that he serves the State and advances the ideology or the cause. The individual is not thought to have a dignity and a fulfillment independent of and finally superior to his function in the State.

In the light of this fundamental position, it becomes clear that the purpose of education is to assist the individual to become an effective and efficient servant of the State or the ideology. The State

---

[6] The very expressive term *brainwashing* has come to be applied to this kind of education.

reserves to itself the right to control both the form and the content of education since education itself has no purpose beyond that allotted to it by the State. The individual is a good citizen to the extent he promotes the cause; his education is good if, through it, he learns how best to promote the cause. The purpose of education is not to encourage independence of judgment, but to assure total immersion in the ideology to the extent that the citizen thinks in all ways and at all times in keeping with the ideological doctrine.

Perhaps the clearest example of how the purpose of education is understood within an ideology and in a country ruled by *the few* is offered by Soviet Russia. David Miller makes this point very clearly in an article in the New York Herald Tribune, Sunday, September 2, 1962, in the section called "The Forum":

> Soviet education, first of all, has a goal indelibly written into its very being. Under the dictum laid down by Lenin, education is a weapon for moving society forward on the road to Communism.
>
> "The content of education," said Lenin, "and in particular, instruction in philosophy, social sciences, and Communist moral education, must be determined solely by the Communist Party."
>
> Soviet leadership since the revolution has used the educational system to serve the State. Since the Party plans all economic and social developments in the Soviet Union, it also determines the nation's educational requirements and the skills needed.
>
> A key point was that effective with the 1962 school year, every Soviet child will receive a minimum of eight years' compulsory schooling instead of seven. School attendance begins at age seven and finishes at fifteen or sixteen.
>
> Beyond that, Soviet education is much more selective than that in the United States. The emphasis in the Soviet Union is on labor training and the bulk of Soviet youths enter employment immediately after completing the basic eight years of school.
>
> What students are taught is theoretically under the control of the Soviet Union's fifteen republics but in practice every aspect of the Soviet school system is essentially planned, directed, and controlled from Moscow.[7]

The situation in Russia is typical rather than exceptional. Education within an ideology is most likely to follow this same pattern. The purpose of education is clear-cut and well defined; it is to further and extend the ideology. This purpose is well understood by

---

[7] David Miller, ". . . And Classes Begin In the Soviet Union," *The New York Herald Tribune* (September 2, 1962), p. 1, Section 2, The Forum, Vol. CXXII.

those who rule and the thought that education might be a good in itself with its own purposes and its own rewards for those who pursue it is never considered. Neither is it considered that the ideology itself should be held up to examination so that it might stand or fall on the weight of the evidence. The purpose of education is to make people faithful, not thoughtful.

Quantity and Quality of Education

In a country ruled by *the few,* education will ordinarily be limited to the few. Basic education may well be offered to all, but, if so, it is for reasons proper to the advancing of the ideology or the cause rather than for the proper good of education or of the person to be educated.

In one sense it is possible to hold that the purposes which education seeks to achieve are the best criteria of the quality or the caliber of the educative processes. In this sense, if the educational system achieves or attains what it sets out to accomplish, then that education is of high quality. It would be of poor quality only if it did not attain the goals or standards set for it.

Judged by this possible criterion, education in a country ruled by *the few* is often of good or even high quality. The aims and purposes of the schools are rigid but precisely set forth. The teachers and instructors have themselves been carefully indoctrinated in party doctrine and the party line, and they know what is expected of them. The pupils and students are not allowed to explore other ideas or to question deeply the ideas presented to them. No pains are spared to expose the students to the ideas they are supposed to accept and hold as valid. On the other hand, students are not made aware of the weaknesses in the ideological system. If other ideas are examined at all, it is only to point out their weaknesses. Consequently, the students emerge from such a system well schooled in what the party or *the few* want them to believe, to think, and to do.

If such is the measure of good education, then it might be said that the quality of education in such a society is high.

But there is another and vastly more important way of measuring the quality of the educational endeavor: Does the education system accomplish at a high level what it objectively should accomplish for each student? Is education doing what education can and should do?

If it can be assumed that there are objective purposes for education, higher and truer than simple indoctrination into a thought system (whether that system be Nazism, Fascism, Communism, or Shinto-ism, or any other), then education is of high quality only if it achieves these objective purposes.

Based on this criterion, education within an ideology is generally of poor quality, indeed. The students are, quite literally, forced to think what they are told to think. The educational system seeks to fill the minds of the students and to close them, not to open them. Individual enrichment and fulfillment are regarded as unimportant; great emphasis is placed on conformity, submissiveness, and ac-quiescence. There is no room for creativity. The teachers regard the truth as already at hand and pre-established (e.g., in the works of Marx and Lenin) so that teaching becomes a matter of commmen-tary, statement, or exposition rather than one of inquiry and dis-covery.

If education is esteemed as a way of weighing the evidence and arriving at independent and free judgment, then any education aimed directly at indoctrination in an ideology is poor and faulty. Its quality is necessarily and totally inferior because in its very process it renders free judgment impossible. The primary value in such a system is acceptance and passivity in the intellectual order, although the ideology sets out to instill in the students a crusading zeal for the cause as well. In fact, the entire educational system in an ideology might be said to be action-centered because it involves a program to be carried out and not ideas to be thought through.

Direct Influences in the Classroom

The correlation between types of political organization and the educational system is clearly seen in the classrooms themselves. Again, these influences can best be considered by examining two aspects: curriculum and methods of teaching.

Curriculum. In a country or society in which rule is by *the few,* the school curriculum will reflect the interests and the thinking of that few. Scientific and technological studies, since they pose no direct threat to the ideology, may very well flourish, though even this is not always the case. An ideology, not in itself a friendly en-vironment for basic scientific research, will sometimes honor and reward its scientists and allow them free scope in order to use their accomplishments as a proof of the validity of the ideology. There might be heavy emphasis on those subjects or disciplines which are practical and pragmatic and those which are related to business and industry. In an advanced society dominated by an ideology, there will be great need for persons who are skilled and semiskilled and provision must be made for this kind of education. Education in and for the military is almost always prominent.

But those areas of knowledge which have to do with human life and the human spirit will be tightly controlled and circumscribed. Each ideology, for example, will have its own stance on the question of teaching religion in the schools. History will be rewritten and taught from the particular perspective of the ideology. Those men and those movements which seem to favor the ideology will be stressed, glorified, and exaggerated. Those which do not favor it will not even be discussed. Thus history ceases to be an objective study and becomes a kind of mythology or a vehicle for persuasion or promotion.

Similarly, literature, the social studies, and the fine arts lose their critical role and become means for furthering the cause.[8] Only those themes in literature which are "acceptable" are discussed. The social sciences are used as ways of extolling the existing economic and political system and showing the advantages of the present form of social and political organization. In like manner, the expressions of the human heart and soul in the fine arts—music, painting, ballet, sculpture—must meet and conform with the dictates of the party line. In all these areas the greatest crime is deviation or derogation, and the artist is judged not by his art but by how his art contributes to and advances the ideology.

Methods of teaching. Methods of teaching are, of course, determined largely by the teacher's understanding and his attitudes toward that which is to be taught. How does he interpret his profession

---

[8] "To this Socialist realist method two other principles have been added, which Soviet writers and artists are supposed to observe. The first is *partiinost,* which means partymindedness, obedience to the party line. The second is *narodnost,* which means acceptance of the Leninist dictum that 'art belongs to the people,' and is created for the people.

The uninspired application of these principles has had the effect of turning poems into rhymed slogans and paintings into political placards." Mark Frankland, "Khrushchev Faces a Khrushchevian Dilemma," *The New York Times Magazine* (May 12, 1963), 80. Copyright by *The New York Times.* Reprinted by permission.

and what does he hope to achieve in his teaching? What is his role in society? Method and content are not, in fact, separable. But several characteristics of actual teaching methods follow closely from the total environment in which the teacher finds himself.

In a society ruled by *the few,* there is little value attached to originality and creativity. The fundamental concepts of the ideology are the same for all and even the ordering and arranging of these concepts is not likely to be left to the individual teacher. Decisions about what is to be taught, when, and how, will be official political decisions and not professional decisions.

For this reason, teaching will be relatively standardized and uniform. The teacher will spend most time in *telling* the students and this means some variation, depending on school level, of what has come to be known as the lecture method. Teaching will consist of exposition rather than exploration or even explanation. The teachers will be teaching, for the most part, out of the assumption that all the important ideas and forms of knowledge are already known. His task is to make sure the students absorb these ideas. Since the curriculum is much more in the nature of a blueprint to be assigned, imposed, and accepted than it is in the nature of an open-ended intellectual experience, the teaching methods will be directed toward presenting the blueprint in the safest and swiftest way.

It follows, then, that the students will be expected to do a great deal of memorizing. The teacher will be a kind of director of the memorization process. He will supervise the students' efforts both by giving clear-cut assignments and by assuring himself that the students have furnished the "right" answers. There will be great reliance on authoritative pronouncements and the teacher will be regarded as the authority. There will not be much drama in the teaching-learning process or much personal interchange between teacher and student.

Furthermore, the teaching will tend to be largely verbal and intellectualized. But since the purpose of the teaching will be to secure a commitment to the ideology from the student, there will be frequent emotional appeals as well. The party and the cause almost become objects of worship. The student's personal interests, needs, aptitudes, and desires will be thought of as insignificant in the light of the great cause he is to serve. There will be virtually no interest in individual differences and no attempt to develop them.

CHAPTER IV

Education and Rule by The Many

The term *rule by the many* might be somewhat confusing. Aristotle used it as a way of differentiating those governments, political systems, or types of rule in which ruling power was widespread among the free citizens of a city or a country. It is not likely that even Aristotle understood the full dimension and applications of the concept, since in his time the right to vote and to hold office was limited to those persons who were not slaves, to property holders and educated people, and to men. Aristotle did not make any provision in his classification of types of rule for what might be called *rule by all*. Universal suffrage would not have been known to him. But in a very real sense the concept of rule by *the many* extends to, and includes, rule *by all*.

Even in Aristotle's time there were numerous cities which conducted their political affairs on the basis of a constitution in the framing of which many persons, rather than only one or a few, had a voice. Decisions about eligibility and qualifications for office, about tenure of office, about legislative and judicial procedures, and about ways and means of promoting the common good were based on the joint thinking of *the many* rather than on the isolated thinking of *the one* or *the few*. To this type of organization Aristotle gave the name *democracy*. It was assumed a democracy was much more likely than any other form of government to operate in the public interest since the views of *the many* would help in shaping its final decisions. The term *mobocracy*, meaning mob rule, has been coined to indicate the breakdown of organized government and to suggest the chaotic condition resulting when *the many* attempt to rule without purpose, direction, or control.

The basis of Aristotle's thinking was partly historical, though it was also largely rational and humanistic. Democracy seemed to work and to give more people a chance to find happiness and dignity by providing the means by which they could share in rule and government. It seemed to be supported by the law of reason or the natural law. It remained for the Christian concept of man, however, to introduce into political theory the idea that each human being has a unique and personal relationship to God and an eternal worth and destiny that followed from that relationship. This idea gave a solid theoretical basis and meaning to the notion of individual and personal freedom. The person could no longer regard himself or be regarded as a servant of the State or simply as a passive instrument for carrying out the wishes of others. His rights and responsibilities as a person came not from man but from God, and therefore his life-interests were higher than the interests of any separate State. In this sense, he was the equal of every other person alive.

Rule by *the many* or rule by *all* might better be called rule by *the individual* or rule by *the individual person*. The person never gets lost in the multitude and rule by *the many* never permits the individual to justify indifference to the political order on the ground that his is just one vote. The right to rule—the power of governing —is a power delegated to the State by the individual person. The State has no power other than that given to it by each of the persons in society. There is no right to govern except that given by the consent of those governed. Rule by *the many* rests fundamentally on the concept that each person is potentially capable—and has the right and the responsibility—to share in those decisions which are going to affect his freedom and his life. It also rests on the theory that no one is better able to look after a man's interests than that man himself. He may fail, to be sure, but so might anyone else who assumed authority over him.

Rule by *the many,* or democracy, should never be thought of simply as extending decision-making power to larger numbers of people. It rests on a profound realization of the importance of each individual and his right to determine for himself how he will fulfill himself as a human being in the light of all his obligations: to God, to family, to society, and to himself. And since man is a rational and a political animal, he must come to understand his important duties as a citizen and as a cooperating and participating member of society.

The Contemporary World Scene

Rule by *the many* is still a relatively new concept. Universal suffrage is a product of the present generation. The idea that government should be of, by, and for the people had a brief moment of glory in ancient Greece but, both prior to that time and for long after, democracy was neither known nor practiced. The long history of the human race in all parts of the world has been written, by and large, in the records of one form or another of rule by *the one* or rule by *the few* rather than rule by *the many*.

An appraisal of either the status or the stability of democracy in the contemporary world, for purposes of this study, must be made in general terms. It would be impossible to consider the situation in each individual democratic country, but certain generalizations are both possible and valuable.

The first such generalization would be this: In our day, the idea of democracy has captured to a profound degree the imaginations of peoples all over the world. In a way never before thought possible, the twentieth century has given rise to a worldwide blossoming of the democratic spirit. What had a century or two earlier been regarded as an improbable experiment has now become, at least in theory, a universally admired and respected mode of political organization. This worldwide movement was well advanced at the time of World War I, when the rallying slogan was "Make the world safe for democracy."

The terms *democracy* and *republic* have become virtually synonymous. Practically all the member countries of United Nations, and especially is this true of all the newer member countries, refer to themselves as *republics*. The term *republic* is a general term used to indicate a type of government or a mode of political organization in which sovereign ruling power resides with and derives from the people themselves. In a republic, the ruling power is exercised by elected delegates who are directly responsible to the electorate. Although it is most common for modern States which have this form of government to call themselves simply *republics,* some States qualify the term by calling themselves *peoples' republics,* or *federal republics,* or *independent republics.*

To use the word *republic* is to indicate a high degree of delegation of power. Government in most modern States could not be carried on at all if there were not extensive delegation and representation. The word *democracy* does not have the same explicit connotation because theoretically democracy could function without delegation of authority. A republic could not. But both *republic* and *democracy* imply that rule is in the hands of the people, in the hands of *the many*. Representatives always act in the name of the people and by their right; they do not have any other authority.

One of the curious developments in modern times is that some countries in which rule is obviously by *the one* or by *the few* choose to call themselves *republics* or *democracies*. Some go through the pretense of elections, though there are no issues and no choices. There is only one slate of candidates. The people merely sign their name or mark their ballot and the rulers interpret this formality as a sign of approval. The people do not even have the option of refusing to vote; they are forced to go to the polls.

The second generalization would be this: Modern democracies or republics range on a scale from those which are highly developed, though by no means perfect, to those which are just emerging and which need careful nurturing if they are to survive at all. The surge toward democracy on the part of peoples all over the world is the result of many factors and forces. But a sudden movement from a primitive and in many ways apolitical or nonpolitical condition to a condition of democratic self-government is fraught with danger. Democracy just does not function gratuitously; it must be prepared and planned. It needs educated personnel and high-quality leadership. Yet more democracies have come into existence since World War II, a period of less than twenty years, than existed before it. A faltering democracy is an open invitation to usurpation of power by a dictator.

In a democracy, progress and improvement are necessary. Even those democracies which are highly developed and experienced in democratic forms and procedures must be constantly searching for the means to perfect them. They must realize that the right to vote is the beginning and not the end of democratic action. Those democracies which are just emerging have the great, but not insurmountable, problem of putting their democracies on a firm theoretical and practical basis. This involves growing accustomed to the use of reason and persuasion in the matter of settling differences of ideas and attitudes; it involves finding and educating public-spirited executives, administrators, and civil servants; it involves raising the standards of living and the levels of culture to the point where the citizens have the leisure, the knowledge, and the inclination to concern themselves with the affairs of political rule.

In this connection an especially perplexing problem arises. Understandably, the temptation will be for the emerging democracies to seek counsel and assistance from those democracies which are already firmly established. In turn, the democracies already established will be eager to share the benefits of their experience and their hard-won triumphs with the emerging democracies. And no doubt there are many ways in which such assistance can be extremely valuable. But there is a danger that the forms of democracy appropriate to peoples with one cultural background and tradition will not be suitable to those of another. Some principles of democratic action will be applicable in all times and in all human situations; but there are certain basic understandings, certain modes of operation, a certain élan, certain traditions, and a certain community of living that cannot be readily transferred from one culture to another. If democracy is to be permanent and meaningful, each country and each culture must work out its own form. And it could well be that in the struggle for democracy and in the inevitable experimentation that must take place, the emerging democracies will bring to light ideas and practices from which the older democracies might well benefit.

The third generalization is this: the very survival of democracy as a form of government is being challenged throughout the world in a most powerful and essential way. It is being challenged on many fronts—the military, the economic, the sociopolitical—but most fundamentally in the realm of ideas. The Cold War is a war of ideas, and the Constitution of UNESCO is correct when it says that the modern struggle is a struggle for the minds of men. This struggle is made even more complex by the fact that, as has been pointed out, both sides claim the word *democracy* as their own.

Democracy has always led and probably always will lead a precarious existence. It is never finally and firmly achieved, and it is threatened both from within and from without. However, the mid-twentieth century enemy of democracy is something new and profoundly different. It is the Marxist or Communist system of thought which views man as an economic unit and which places his value totally in his ability to produce and consume. Under such a system, freedom and human dignity become meaningless. Man is a mere unit in a master plan designed by the Party and by the State. Communism does not challenge just this or that phase of democratic theory. It challenges its very essence in challenging its concept of the meaning of man.

Economists outside the Communist orbit deny the validity of Communism even as an economic system. Non-Communist philosophers deny that a system of thought and life dominated by economic theory can give rise to meaningful, lasting, or satisfying spiritual or humanistic values. Nonetheless, the conditions of the twentieth century—rapid industrialization, scientific advancements, the population explosion, the grinding poverty of large segments of the world's population, the uprooting and dislocation of whole peoples, and the emergence of strong and convinced leaders at a time they were eagerly sought—have fostered the growth of Communism. Roughly one half of the world's population is Communist-dominated. This adherence to the Communist philosophy and system has been won through a combination of promises of economic security and sheer force.

Whether democracy will survive or not depends to a large extent on how well the democratic countries can hold to the primacy and the importance of the spiritual values of liberty and their concept of the meaning of the life of man and his dignity; how effectively they can compete in the marketplace and, if necessary, on the battlefield; and how valid and genuine is the process of education in those countries which now carry the responsibility for, and the hopes for, democracy.

Attitudes Toward Education

Those countries or cultures in which rule is by *the many*—the democracies—must inevitably enter into a close partnership and alliance with the educational effort. So close in fact will this alliance be and so mutually interdependent is the relationship between rule by *the many* and education that they might almost be considered to be different aspects of the same thing. Democracy is unworkable and even unthinkable unless it is conjoined with a strong and free educational system. Education is the means by which *the many* become qualified to rule themselves and to share and participate in governing. At the very founding of the American republic, Thomas Jefferson pointed out that it is impossible for men to be both free and ignorant.

The attitude of a democratic people toward education is most favorable and encouraging, but it is somewhat weak. Democracy depends on education and cannot live long or well without it. Conversely, education itself finds its fullest flowering in an environment created by that mode of political organization in which rule is by *the many*. There is a tendency on the part of some, however, to regard education as a panacea for all the ills and shortcomings of democracy and of life in general. "More education" is the answer to every problem. The position is valid if education is all-embracing and includes spiritual and moral values as well as intellectual values, but not if it simply means staying in school longer. A good education can and should be the gateway to a good life. But this raises the question of how one teaches such things as honor, honesty, discipline, faith, humility, and humor.

Perhaps the easiest way to discover why the attitude of a democracy toward education must be one of close affinity and natural support is to view the matter from two viewpoints: that of the government or ruling body and that of the governed.

It will also be helpful to see this matter in a related but quite distinct way by considering the good of the individual and that of society itself.

In a democracy the government is not a group or an entity apart from and removed from the people themselves. In a genuine sense the government *is* the people. In a democracy the government will be intensely interested in education and favorable toward it. It will realize its success as a government depends on how accurately and intelligently the citizens can interpret the policies and programs it proposes to them. It will realize that many important decisions depend on long-range views rather than on short-term, emotional, and uninformed opinions. The government must have the support and cooperation of the people. Steady and reliable cooperation can only be based on the best intelligence and best information available. The government will not long be able to conceal its own ineptitude, if that should be the case, or its lack of faith and confidence in the people.[1]

---

[1] There is profound wisdom, as well as good democratic theory of government, in Abraham Lincoln's oft-quoted comment: "You can fool all of the people some of the time and some of the people all the time, but you can't fool all the people all the time."

The government knows it must frequently rely on the judgments of experts and that the educational system must give rise to some men of extraordinary capacity. The government knows, too, that it must be able to communicate easily and quickly with the citizens both before and after an action is taken. If the need for decisive action arises, the government will want the citizens to understand the reasons for immediate action and the grounds of the subsequent explanation. The government will want the citizens educated so that it can operate effectively and so that the decisions to be made by the citizens, including the basic decision of whether to continue this particular government in office, will be in the country's best interests.

Similarly, the governed—the people themselves—will strongly support and favor education. One of education's prime tasks is to help form each person into a responsible citizen. Responsible citizens realize that the welfare of the State depends in a large measure on their own intelligence and on the intelligence and the good will of those whom they choose as leaders. They will realize, further, that the strength of a democracy depends on a kind of unity and solidarity that comes from the effort of all concerned to help make the democracy work well. Systematic intelligence must be brought to bear on both the problems and the promises of their democracy.

The citizens will know that their personal participation in the democracy will be more meaningful and valuable if it is informed and well reasoned; they will want to contribute good ideas of their own and share in the good ideas of others. They will know that the quality of the democracy itself depends upon the quality of each individual's participation in it. Cooperation in decision-making, too, implies communication of ideas, and such communication is possible only among persons who have shared basic educational experiences. Finally, all persons in a democracy will desire education for themselves and others as a way of coming to appreciate freedom and of learning how best to use that freedom in the enrichment of human life. One of the great values of democratic life is the increase of respect, among the citizens, for one another.

The second approach to understanding the highly favorable regard in which democratic countries hold education is based on an analysis of the individual good and the common good.

Both democratic theory and educational theory are deeply committed to the importance of assisting the individual person to attain his true and proper good and goal in life. In this they reinforce and complement each other. Democratic countries will view education as a primary means by which the individual achieves realization and fulfillment. Not all persons in a democracy will necessarily agree on what the final and best good of the person is: some will hold it to be based on the immortality of the soul of man and his relation to God; others will hold it to consist of a life of culture and the enjoyment of the life of the mind and spirit; others will see it as a life of unselfish service and dedication to some important cause; others will see it simply as a life of triumphing over problems and enjoying the pleasures of friendship, love, and resourcefulness. But the root of all democratic theory is the belief that man has a personal and a private good. He is not simply a social organism. He is not simply a unit in a collective group or one of a herd. He is not, in fact, just a citizen. He has a life, a soul, and a good of his own. In the very process of attaining his personal good he becomes a better citizen.

Democracy gives its full endorsement and approval to the process of education because of its concern for the good of the individual person. But both democracy and education are also necessarily interested in the common good, the good of all. Here, too, their roles are complementary.

The idea of the common good is not just a metaphor or even a logical mental construct. It is not just a juridical device. Each society has a common good as real as, though subordinate to, the personal good of each individual. The common good is both more than and different from the sum total of the individual goods of all the citizens. It consists of all those aspects of life which persons share in common and which are necessary to a high level of group or societal organization. The promotion of the common good is a duty of both democracy and education, and education is one of the main means used by democracy for promoting the common good.

Man does not simply tolerate group life, as if it were an appendage to his own personal life. He is immersed in it and it is essential to his nature even as man. At the minimum level, the common good provides for the protection of the rights of all members of the society. But this protection is not the realization of the common good; it serves only to create the proper conditions so that all members of society can share in those goods which can be achieved only in and by society. The common good thus extends to the spiritual, intellectual, cultural, moral and social, physical and recreational, and political goods as well as the economic good. A basic fallacy of Communism is that it gives primary importance to the material and economic aspects of the common good and it denies freedom to the individual in the name of the common good.

The good of the person and the common good are not mutually exclusive. The person achieves his own good through participating in the common good. On the other hand, the common good is achieved only insofar as each person contributes to it and shares in it. The proper understanding of the common good makes it possible to avoid the individualism which destroys the life of society and the collectivism which destroys the life of the person. Democracy looks to education to help it create and maintain this balance. In doing so, democracy places education among its highest concerns.

Purpose of Education

There are various meanings to the question: Does education in a democracy have a purpose? Since education is a human activity or process, and since little, if any, rational human activity is completely random or arbitrary, education is sure to have some purpose. The more significant question is this: In a democracy does the process of education have a purpose or an objective over and above and outside the democratic process itself? Or: Does democratic theory assign a purpose to education so that the educational process can be planned and directed toward the achievement of that purpose? Or put yet another way: Does democratic theory leave it up to the educative process itself to decide whether it has any purposes and what these will be?

However the question is worded, it is a crucial one. Its answer entails the whole matter of how much or how little planning and guiding of the educational process there is to be. Is education in a democracy to be thought of as an architectonic, a purposeful and substantive building toward an end, or as a process, the direction of which changes as circumstances unfold?

In countries ruled by *the one* and by *the few*, education has its purposes set for it as clearly as does, for example, business, the theatre, or the military. In a free and democratic society, one ruled by *the many,* it is the people themselves who determine whether education is to have any comprehensive purpose and what that purpose is to be.[2]

The broad question of the purpose of education in a democracy is, of course, closely related to the question of whether democracy —or for that matter, life itself—has any set purpose. But these questions are not precisely to the point in the present discussion.

Some philosophers of education maintain that, in a democracy, the process of education takes its clue from democratic theory and is experimental, openended, and ongoing. There are ends in view but no over-all or ultimate ends. Education is not without purpose but its purposes are within and part of the educative process. In this thinking, the principal purpose for education would be to provide a satisfying response to the felt needs of the students and of the society. John Dewey, perhaps the most influential American philosopher of education, wrote in his classic work on this point:

> Since growth is the characteristic of life, education is all one with growing; it has no end beyond itself. The criterion of the value of school education is the extent in which it creates a desire for continued growth and supplies means for making the desire effective in fact.[3]

Thus, Dewey and those who followed his thinking found the purpose of education in growth. Since growth is the ultimate goal, there is no point in asking: "Growth toward what?" Nor is there any sure way of determining in advance whether a particular process will produce growth in a particular student.

This position gained wide acceptance, not only in America, but

---

[2] An illustration, drawn from an altogether different order of discourse, of what an over-all purpose of education would be is that taken from the encyclical of Pope Pius XI, *Christian Education of Youth.* In one place he writes: "In fact since education consists essentially in preparing man for what he must be and for what he must do here below, in order to attain the sublime end for which he was created, it is clear that there can be no true education which is not wholly directed to man's last end."

In another place he writes: "The proper and immediate end of Christian education is to cooperate with divine grace in forming the true and perfect Christian." Pope Pius XI, *Christian Education of Youth,* Encylical (New York: The Paulist Press, n.d.).

[3] This quotation from John Dewey's *Democracy and Education* was selected for inclusion in *John Dewey: Dictionary of Education,* edited by Ralph B. Winn (New York: Philosophical Library, Inc., 1959), pp. 50–51.

also throughout the world among those philosophers of education who were trying, perhaps too hard, to make sure that education in a democracy could not be accused of any form of indoctrination. Though this position is still firmly held in many circles, it has less acceptance today. Its tendency is to protect a purist and rather naïve concept of democracy and to eviscerate education.

This study does not seek to resolve the basic philosophical question of whether there is, or must be, a democratic theory of education which follows from, and corresponds to, democratic theory itself. If there were such, that theory would include a statement of purpose for education in a democracy. But it is not apparent that any law of inner consistency would require such a theory. On the other hand, the pluralist principle of democracy points to the conclusion that in a democracy there well might be several equally tenable interpretations of the ultimate purpose of education. None of these would conflict with democratic theory and each, in turn, could strengthen it.

But inner consistency does demand that all education in a democracy have at least this one basic purpose: to assist in making it possible for democracy to function properly. Nothing could be more fundamental or more urgent. Education may have purposes and objectives other than this and even higher than this, but at the very least it has this purpose. Quite clearly, education in a democracy should not be at cross purposes with the system of which it is a vital and integral part.

This broad purpose of education in a democracy contains two equally important elements: to make the necessary knowledge available to all citizens and to inculcate in all the citizens a value system appropriate for a democracy.

The effective functioning of a democracy presupposes that the citizens will be informed and knowledgeable. It is, of course, difficult to state unequivocally how much knowledge or even what kinds of knowledge are necessary for a democracy to function smoothly and with strength. But a basic purpose of education in a democracy is to see to it that whatever knowledge is necessary is available at the proper time and in the proper way. The knowledge requirements for a democracy are vastly different in times of international stress and crisis than they would be in times of relative calm. Similarly, they are much different in an age of scientific advancement or space exploration than they would have been in a more agrarian or humanistic age.[4] But at all times and under all conditions democracy demands a level of sophistication and knowledge far greater than that which would be demanded in a country ruled by *the one* or *the few*.

Democratic rule implies that *the many* have the right to vote and to share in decision-making. Intelligent exercise of the right to vote and to discuss issues freely requires a background of knowledge and of education. If the decisions arrived at in the democratic process are frivolous or immature because of lack of knowledge, democracy becomes an easy prey of the man with the strong idea and the strong arm. Voting and deciding mean genuine discernment among possible alternatives. Voting is not just a means for registering emotion; it should be a deliberate action requiring careful thought and accurate judgment. If it is true that education in a democracy has the purpose of assisting that democracy to function properly, then education should provide for the power of the ballot to be balanced by the power of knowledge and trained intelligence.

Since the life of man in society is not simply a life of ideas but also of values, feelings, and attitudes, a second purpose of education in a democracy is to assist each person to discover and to make his own those values which are essential to democratic functioning. How education can best inculcate values is not the question at the moment. Valuing is much more a matter of experiencing than it is of intellectual knowing, and education must seek ways of helping students to experience the values inherent in and necessary to democracy. The values held by a person or a society are not without intellectual content, but a value differs from an idea in that it requires an emotional commitment as well. Each person has an implicit scale of values: some things are highly valued, others only moderately so. In a democratic society, democracy itself should be

---

[4] As Mr. C. P. Snow so dramatically points out in his book, *The Two Cultures and the Scientific Revolution* (New York: Cambridge University Press, 1959), one of the most pressing demands for knowledge in modern democracies is the knowledge of how to bridge the almost complete gap now existing between the scientists who know little of the humanistic and the humanists who know nothing of science. To know how to understand and cope with the scientific revolution requires some depth of knowledge of both science and humanity. Perhaps a whole new concept of education must emerge which will make it possible for the democracies to educate scientific humanists and humanistic scientists.

highly valued by all the citizens. Education helps not only in pointing out why democracy should be valued highly but also in bringing the value of democracy to fruition and completion in commitment and action.

Democracy itself is a high value. But as a system it is a complex of many values, each of which plays a part in the general system and each of which is a concern of education. At one level, for example, democracy places high value on freedom and on the life and person of the individual. At another level, democracy values the participation and cooperation of all persons. At still another level, democracy values a spirit of patience with minor inefficiencies and a willingness to compromise where possible. Democracy also values an openness to new ideas and to the testing of them. And democracy values the long-range test of results rather than the short-range test.

Without a widespread commitment to these and other values, democracy cannot function properly. If a person does not see any value in participating in the decision-making process, he will neither contribute the benefit of his knowledge and experience to the process nor be moved to cooperate in carrying out the decision. If all persons were indifferent and refused to participate, there could be no democracy. Or, if a person values security and efficiency more than he does freedom, he might be disposed to allow others, who promised him these values, to make his decisions for him.

Values, like ideas, are the product of the learning process. Values are not innate or acquired at birth. If democracy is to work successfully, those values on which it is based must become part of the purpose and program of education. An outline of the fundamental values on which democracy might be securely based and with which education in a democracy might wisely concern itself is suggested by the eminent French philosopher, Jacques Maritain. He writes:

> Modern civilization is a worn-out venture; it is not a question of sewing on patches here and there, but of a total and substantial reformation, a trans-valuation of its cultural principles; since what is needed is a change to the primacy of quality over quantity, of work over money, of the human over technical means, of wisdom over science, of the common service of human beings instead of

the covetousness of unlimited individual enrichment or a desire in
the name of the State for unlimited power.[5]

Quantity and Quality of Education

Quantity. It is impossible to put in any exact formula the
amount of education necessary to the efficient operation of a democratic society. Education is not a quantum as, for example, a kilo-
watt-hour is. "Years of schooling" is a most misleading measure of
education. The principle that all the people must be educated and
that they must be educated at least to the point where it is possible
for them to be active, participating, and responsible citizens is clear.
In a democracy no one is excluded from the right to vote on the
basis of color, sex, religion, or national background. Neither is any
otherwise qualified citizen excluded from holding office on any of
these counts. It follows then that education will have to be universal,
to extend to all citizens. Whether attendance at school should be
mandatory and, if so, for what length of time will have to be decided by each particular democracy. Whether, for example, formal
education through elementary school, through secondary school,
through college, or through eighteen or twenty-two years of life is
necessary must be determined in the light of specific historical and
cultural conditions. But a democracy cannot function well in the
modern world if all the citizens do not have at least a fundamental
and general education.[6]

Discussions of the amount of education necessary in a democracy
frequently stop short of an important factor. They measure a man's
education by the number of years he has been in school. They do
not take into account education which occurs after formal schooling is completed. But education in a democracy must necessarily

[5] Jacques Maritain, *True Humanism,* 6th ed. (New York: Charles Scribner's
Sons, 1954), p. 201. Translated by M. R. Adamson.

[6] This ideal is still far from attainment even in the most advanced democracies.
The United States of America has always placed great stress on education. Yet the
United States Commissioner of Education reports, according to an Associated
Press dispatch dated May 17, 1963, that 25 million Americans over eighteen years
of age have completed only eight years of schooling. This total includes 8 million
adults over twenty-five years of age who have completed fewer than five years of
schooling and are considered functionally illiterate. Thus, roughly between one-
fifth and one-sixth of the Americans over eighteen years of age have completed
only eight years of schooling. And approximately one out of each twenty Americans over twenty-five years of age is functionally illiterate.

be a lifelong and continuing education. Whether schooling is thought of as "life" or as a preparation for life, it is never possible to assign an end or a limit to the educational process. No one can say he has had a "sufficient" quantity of education. New discoveries, new theories, new processes, and new problems are constantly emerging and one's education must keep pace with them if he is to take a responsible part in making the decisions these changes force on society. Formal education in a democracy is clearly a way of making it possible for a man to continue his education throughout his lifetime.

The more advanced democracies have already made great progress in providing formal means for continuing education. In some communities there are as many adults in schools of one kind or another as there are youngsters. Some formal continuing education is supplied by the school system, some by business and industry, some by the colleges and universities, and some by the social and recreational agencies. And, of course, the informal means of continuing education in a democracy—the mass media, the law itself, the political party organizations, and the educative efforts of both management and labor unions, for example—are part of the very atmosphere of democracy.

Quality. Democracy aims not only at making education available but also at making the best possible education available. The word *quality* implies in education, as elsewhere, standards of measurement and evaluation. Since education is such a personal matter and since it involves the depths of the human spirit, it is difficult to find objective criteria by which to judge its quality. Further, what might be generally agreed to be high-quality education for one student or group of students might not be such for another. Quality in education requires bringing to each student the kind of education best for him.

Perhaps the best and most general answer is that education is good to the extent that it is meaningful to the student—meaningful not only as a response to his felt and immediate needs but also in the total context of his mind, his soul, and his life. Education need not be child-centered in that the student's wants and interests direct the process. The subject matters make their own rigid demands and society's interests are as important as the child's. But there is no escaping the fact that the child or the student is the center of the educational process; unless the process has meaning for him, it is wasted.

High-quality education implies a well-prepared and dedicated faculty, an interested and eager student body, adequate facilities and equipment for carrying out the educational task, a thoughtfully adapted curriculum, and a total environment conducive to effective teaching and learning. But the final and only real criterion of the quality of the educational process is the meaning which the student finds in his education. To the extent he perceives the meaning of what he is studying and the implications and applications of this study to the world of ideas and of practical affairs, the pupil or student will be receiving a good education. To be good, education must be relevant, vital, and stimulating.

The quality of a democracy depends on the quality of education in that democracy. Life in a democracy is meaningful only if the educational process is meaningful.

Direct Influences in the Classroom

The democratic spirit and the democratic mode of political organization will have direct, strong, and immediate influences in the classrooms of a culture or country. These influences can be recognized in at least three distinct forms: in the role of the teacher, in the activities and the attitudes of the students, and in the general climate of learning.

The role of the teacher. Teachers in a democracy will tend to have a profound sense of responsibility and a feeling for the importance of their profession. A democracy will, in turn, honor its teachers as among its most valued citizens. The teachers realize that the strength and vitality of a democracy as well as the happiness and success of their individual students depend to a large extent on how well they carry out their roles as teachers. Implicit at all times is the thought that some of the youngsters sitting in their classrooms will be the leaders of tomorrow's society. All of these youngsters will have, through the power of the vote, the final and decisive voice about the directions in which the country will move. The ideas and the values the teachers impart to their students will largely shape the world in which both the teachers and the students will one day live.

The teachers will also feel a sense of pride in the important professional work they are performing in society and for it. They will know their contribution to society is both deep and lasting. As teachers, they too are free citizens in a democratic society. They regard themselves as human beings, not as machines or robots transmitting ideas they are forced to teach and into the shaping of which they have put none of their own thinking and spirit. Rather, they regard themselves as artists who have chosen a most difficult and most rewarding form of art. The teaching art requires the best of their creative effort and talent. Teachers in a democracy tend to be independent thinkers, dedicated and happy in their profession.

Democracy makes it possible for the teacher to fulfill to the utmost the essential meaning of teaching. Teaching is not simply the passing out of information presumed to be factual. The concept of teaching is that one who is learned stands in a unique personal relationship—mind to mind and *cor ad cor*—with those who have not yet learned. The teacher systematically brings his own best thinking, his knowledge, his insights, his interpretations, to his students. On the basis of what he has come to know and believe and as the result of his study, reflection, and experience, he lays claim to the full attention of his students. His right to claim the title *teacher* rests on the fact that he knows and is able and willing to help others come to know.

The teacher does not impose his ideas on his students. They are human beings with minds of their own. But it is by means of the teacher's ideas that the student learns and eventually draws his own conclusions. The old question: Should the teacher teach the students *what* to think or should he teach them *how* to think? misses the point. The teacher teaches the student what he (the teacher) thinks and in so doing he teaches the student how to think and opens up to him the possibility of thinking for himself.

In his role, the teacher inspires, encourages, corrects. He teaches by word and by example. The students respect the teacher for what he knows and for how he arrived at what he knows. The teacher is a liaison or a mediator between the world of ideas and values and the minds and the lives of the students. Teaching is always a work of the person, and genuine teaching is the result of one's own personal work with ideas.

The good teacher respects the individual integrity, the freedom, and the conscience of each student. He maintains rigorous standards of intellectual honesty for himself and for his students. He teaches with a good heart in a context of love for the students and regard for the demands of the discipline.

The activities and the attitudes of the students. The students, too, in a democracy will have a high seriousness of purpose in pursuing their education. They will see their education not only as a quest for the guiding ideas and principles of human existence but also as the door to opportunity and significant service in the practical order. The students will expect to share and cooperate in the learning process in much the same way as they share, both now and later, in the democratic process. Life in the school and classroom is life with a particular purpose but it reflects the attitudes of the democratic society of which it is a part.

Through their experiences in the classroom, the students will come to understand that theirs is an open society. Their participation in its life and movements will be only as valuable as the force and clarity of the ideas and the depth of spirit they bring to it. They will respond eagerly to the opportunity to develop their talents and they will discover new talents and new interests. They will quickly realize that society provides them with an education both for their own sake and for the sake of society. Their appreciation of the meaning of freedom and the need for responsibility will be both a direct and an indirect effect of their school and classroom experience.

In the classroom, the student will soon become aware of the fact that his teacher is there to help him. In this, the teacher represents society at large. Neither the teacher nor society is an enemy of the student but, rather, a friend helping him to mature, to express himself, and to realize himself. The student will be inspired to give his best efforts and he will find intense satisfaction in so doing. He will respond to the encouragement he receives and he will be stimulated by the contributions he makes. Because he will be treated as an honored and valuable member of the school and classroom society, he will come to regard himself in that light, and he will, in turn, regard others in the same light. He will find delight, drama, and adventure in the awakening of his intellectual powers, in coming to think for himself, and in working toward the solution of the problems he encounters.

The general climate of learning. The climate of learning in the classrooms in a democratic society will be, as it is in the society itself, an open and unoppressive one. The teaching-learning process will be cooperative rather than competitive; it will be active rather than passive. The student will be urged to explore, to challenge, to check, and to demand proof. The atmosphere will be one in which ideas unfold; they are presented rather than imposed. Inquiry into problems will be encouraged and the acceptance of readymade and pat answers will be discouraged. Learning will not be made easy but it will be made interesting. It will be made clear that the ascertaining of the truth or of the fact is not a matter of vote, nor of popular acceptance, but of how the evidence supports the proposition.

Students will be supported in their efforts at creative and experimental thinking. But due attention will be given to the wisdom of the past and to the heritage and the tradition of ideas. The teacher and the student are necessarily partners in the learning process, but the student is the junior partner and the teacher the senior. The teaching-learning process is not a discussion between or among equals. The child is not the master even in a democracy.

In general, the climate of learning will be permissive and flexible rather than rigid. But laziness, carelessness, and indifference will not be tolerated on the pretext that the primary concern of education is the student and not the subject matter. Genuine learning in a democracy makes greater demands on the student than does the prefabricated learning typical of a society ruled by *the one* or *the few*. Old ideas will not be accepted just because they are old; new ideas will not be accepted just because they are new. A democracy will make every effort to establish an educational climate in which old ideas are open to re-examination and new ideas are explored as they arise. Ideas will be accepted not because they are old or new but only because they are valid.

CHAPTER V

Education and Growth toward Democracy

It has been seen that as an essential function in any society, some form of education will be carried on regardless of the political power structure. But so close is the relationship between the educational process and the system of political rule that education will tend to take on the purposes and characteristics of the particular form of political organization within which it functions. This seems to be almost inevitable. It could well be argued that education should be free of political ties, that its reference is not to political systems or power but to the mind and heart of man. However, the education of man always takes place at a specific point in history and it is always subject to political conditions.

The chapters that follow will concentrate on the relationships between education and that particular form of political organization which has come to be called *democracy*. Democracy merits full consideration for several reasons. As a mode of political organization in which rule is by *the many,* democracy offers the best setting for coming to understand education's full meaning and power. It both relies most heavily on education and gives it fullest freedom to develop in accord with its own inner dynamic principles. It would appear to be the form of government and rule toward which most of the peoples of the world aspire. In a democracy, education serves the purposes of all the people and not just the purposes of *the one* or *the few* who hold political power.

The Bases of Democracy

In order to see clearly how education, properly conceived, aids in the growth and development of democracy, it will be necessary to consider further some of the underlying principles of the theory and practice of democracy. Democratic theory is based on a faith in the fundamental dignity of the individual person and of his fulfillment in freedom. It is also based on a faith in the process of reason as the best and only norm for determining the personal as well as the social or public good.

The democratic faith. In a period of history in which the so-called scientific method, with its demands for exact, rigorous, and empiriological proof, has come to dominate men's thinking and has achieved such spectacular results, the notion that democracy should rest on faith and not on scientific proof is disturbing to many people. Nonetheless, the fact is that democracy requires a bold act of faith in the dignity and value of man and of man's freedom and in reason or intellect, not will, as the best and final arbiter of the public interest. In the strictly scientific sense, or even in the broader sense of proof through pragmatic experience, it would be impossible to demonstrate the necessity and the validity of these two principles. Yet if democracy is to work they must be accepted—on faith. It is not a blind or unreasoned act of faith. There is good historical and experiential ground for making it. It is based in part on the success that has been achieved by means of it and in part on the intuitions of common sense.

The act of faith in democracy can be expressed in any number of ways. That it is an act of faith is clear, however, from a statement such as that which appears in the Declaration of Independence: "We hold these truths to be self-evident. That all men are created equal, that all men are endowed by their creator with certain inalienable rights." This is a masterful and classical statement of the democratic faith. To say that certain truths are self-evident is another way of saying that one puts his faith or confidence in them without requiring proof. The Declaration of Independence does not say that we hold it can be scientifically proved that all men are created equal. It cannot be. Rather, it is clearly implied that all who would understand democracy must accept, as an act of faith, the fact that all men are created equal—i.e., that all men, insofar as they are men, share equally in human nature and in the rights of man.

Human dignity. Democracy rests on the faith or on the premise that each individual person rightfully lays claim to an inviolable dignity and that he finds his fullest perfection as a person in freedom and self-determination. Man's dignity is explained in various ways. Some will find its source in the proposition that God created all men in His own image and likeness. Others will find it implicit in man's spiritual capacities to think and to love. Still others will find it amply enough demonstrated in the literature and poetry of the human race and in the deeds of its heroes, sages, and saints and in the record of tragedy and disaster wherever it has been denied.

If each man has an inner dignity, then it follows that no man is subject to or slave to any other man or to any class, race, or State. Each man is born with rights equal to and the same as those of every other man. Also, although he will inevitably be a member of society, his rights are antecedent to, and dominant over, the claims or the rights of the State. There is profound truth in the simple statement "The State exists for man, not man for the State." The question of man's relation to the State would be answered in the same way even in that world community of man, so much discussed by the utopians and idealists, in which there were no separate and individual national States. If this should ever come about, the world-State itself would still exist for man and not man for the world-State.

The fact of man's essential dignity also leads to the conclusion that man finds his fullest development and perfection in freedom. His choices and his decisions must be his own rather than those of someone else. If any man is regarded either as an instrument for carrying out someone else's ideas and wishes or as a slave for carrying out someone else's orders, he is not free and has no fulfillment in and of himself. But if man possesses and enjoys freedom—if he determines for himself what he is to think, what he is to love, what he is to do and what he is to strive for—then his life has dignity and depth. Unless each man holds himself and every other man in high dignity, democracy cannot succeed.

The role of reason.   A second phase of the democratic faith includes a belief in the fundamental rationality of man.

This means a belief that there is a natural and a rational order in things and that man can arrive at this order through his ability to reason and to think. Reason is the controlling factor in life.

Man is not born fully rational but, as man, he is born with a capacity for reason. This is not to say that man is without emotion. On the contrary, some of his richest human experiences will be deeply emotional. The point is that each man and all men are rational, that there is in human affairs a valid appeal from the purely emotional to the order of reason. Neither is it possible for man to be rational at some specific times and emotional at others as if each man were really two men rather than one. Reason and emotion are inextricably bound together in each man and very often emotion will make it difficult to determine where reason lies. But democracy cannot be based on emotion; it must be based on reason. And the rationality of man cannot be proven but only accepted.

The democratic faith requires that both individual life and group life be regarded as basically rational rather than voluntaristic. The order of reason rather than the order of emotions or instincts, wants, wishes, desires, fantasies, and dreams needs to prevail if democracy is to work at all. Only if man is held to be rational can there be agreement on first principles, agreement on deductions and inferences, and significance in the search for objective evidence. If each man interpreted the world strictly in his own way, there could be no point in discussion and no hope for finding a unified and unifying conclusion.

The critical emphasis placed on reason in a democracy, and a prior faith in its reality and validity, does not suggest that all problems in a truly functioning democracy can be resolved by an appeal to reason. Often major decisions will hinge on preferences and attitudes and not on clearly discernible reasons. Often, too, they will have to be based on the more or less reasonable and not on the completely reasonable. Nor does the emphasis on reason imply that man by nature always exercises good reason and good judgment, although education will help him to do so. It does imply that reason is the best and only arbiter. In the practical order there will be few instances in which reason so clearly points the way that even all persons who are trying to be reasonable will arrive at the same conclusions. But it is the appeal to reason rather than to emotion that will be most helpful in resolving practical conflicts and disputes. For example, the principle of majority rule has proven to be a valuable way of getting to action in democracies. If there were no faith in reason, even so elementary a principle would be unworkable. Similarly, democracy often involves compromise, where possible, and compromise is a work of reason.

The democratic promise. Democratic theory requires an act of faith. But it also provides a hope or a promise. Its promise is a new level of civilization and culture, in which the rights and the freedom of each man are protected and advanced and in which each man comes to accept the responsibilities which are a part of his freedom. Democracy seeks a new and integral humanism. Democratic theory holds that it is possible for men to live well together in freedom and with reason as the guideline, pursuing the good of each and the good of all. It is optimistic but not idealistic.

In seeking to fulfill its promise, democracy needs the best ideas, the good will, and the cooperation of all men. It needs the best possible programs and processes of education. It will be intensively aware of the religious aspirations and expressions of all the people and it will understand the connection, as well as the essential differences, between religious faith and the democratic faith.[1] By making it possible for man to be his own master in the political order, democracy also makes it possible for man to pursue those ends which far transcend the political order.

Democracy not Inevitable

In considering the role of education in the movement of men and peoples toward democracy, it is important to note a further fact about the nature of democracy. It is not at all inevitable. It is not any kind of logical or necessary conclusion toward which the line or the cycle of history inescapably leads. Nor is democracy a condition which, once attained, is never lost. Democracy must be won and rewon not only in every period of history but almost literally every day. In fact, it is never wholly achieved at any moment of history; it is never finished, closed, or complete. Democracy is volatile

---

[1] "In modern times an attempt was made to base the life of civilization and the earthly community on the foundation of mere reason—reason separated from religion and from the Gospel. This attempt fostered immense hopes in the last two centuries—and rapidly failed. Pure reason showed itself more incapable than faith of ensuring the spiritual unity of mankind, and the dream of a 'scientific' creed, uniting men in peace and in common convictions about the aims and basic principles of human life and society, vanished in our contemporary catastrophes. In proportion as the tragic events of the last decades have given the lie to the bourgeois rationalism of the 18th and 19th centuries, we have been confronted with the fact that religion and metaphysics are an essential part of human culture, primary and indispensable incentives in the very life of society.

"As a result, it seems likely that, if democracy enters its next historical stage with sufficient intelligence and vitality, a renewed democracy will not ignore religion, as the bourgeois 19th century society, both individualist and 'neutral,' did; and that this renewed, 'personalist' democracy will be of a *pluralistic* type." Jacques Maritain, *Man and the State* (Chicago: University of Chicago Press, 1951), pp. 108–109.

and precarious; it makes great demands on those who would support it and it is a constant rebuke to those who seek to rule and dominate. Part of its very force is in an openness to change, which carries the risks always conjoined with change.

Democracy poses many a peculiar paradox. At the same time that it offers men freedom, it must constantly remind them that freedom is a condition of life rather than the end of life. At the same time that it puts decision-making power in the hands of the people themselves, it is aware that decision-making is not easy and that some men find great security in letting others make their decisions for them. At the same time that it makes it possible for wise and able men to demonstrate their ability and come into positions of leadership, there is the constant danger that incompetent and unworthy men will reach even the highest positions. At the same time that it stresses the vote and the ballot box, it runs the risk that the people will come to regard voting as a burden and a bother. In the fact that democracy is thus paradoxical, it finds both strength and resilience. In the fact that it is full of tensions, it is never easy or sure.

The several paradoxes of democracy are explainable, at least in part, by the fact that democracy must be considered both as a content and as a process. This means that it is both a set or a body of basic pervasive principles and a way of doing things. In reality the content and process of democracy are not separable. The democratic process is one of the underlying principles of democracy and as such is an important part of its content.

Democracy as content. As a content or body of principles or ideas, democracy is based on an interpretation of man as a being who possesses intrinsic dignity, capable of determining—and free to determine—his own destiny. Since, as a content, democracy derives from the nature of man, it is not dependent on any particular form of economic or social order. However, some forms of economic and social order will be more conducive to democracy than others. In very primitive economies, for example, man might be so busy with the basic economic necessities of life as to have no time for even thinking about democracy. On the other hand, those economies with sufficient amounts of reserve capital can provide both the leisure and the education necessary to democracy.

Further, the right to participate in democracy cannot in any way be made dependent on the holding of property. Democracy does not exist for the sake of protecting private property and neither is the possession of property a qualification for participating in democracy. One of man's inalienable rights is his right to private property, but the actual owning or possessing of property is not essential to human nature. Though a man can voluntarily relinquish the exercise of his right to private property, democracy could not exist in a State in which so fundamental a right were denied.

As a content, then, democracy rests on an interlocking series of individual rights and responsibilities, many of which relate directly to the fact that man is a social being.

The underlying rights and responsibilities crucial to democracy have been well formulated in such documents and proclamations as the Magna Charta, the Bill of Rights affixed to the Constitution of the United States, the Atlantic Charter and its statement of the Four Freedoms, and the Charter of the United Nations. These are mentioned simply as outstanding examples of the effort throughout the ages to articulate the basic content of democracy.

Though these various statements have been extremely helpful in clarifying the nature and content of democracy, they are not meant to be final and irrevocable. Each of them uses universal language. The principles enunciated are as general as possible. But as conditions change, so do the needs and the emphasis of the democratic charter. Obviously, for example, the modern age requires new applications and perhaps a further statement of the principles of the democratic charter on a global scale.

An essential element of the nature and meaning of democracy, considered as a content, is the principle of the rule of law rather than the rule of men. Where any one man or any few men rule, their wills and their decisions become the law. But democracy demands that the law itself, into the making of which the best thinking of *the many* have gone, prevail. No man is above the law. So much is this the case that democracy is often called by another name: *constitutionalism*. The affairs of state and the daily lives of the individual are ruled or governed by a constitution which clearly sets forth what the law is. The constitution may be either written or unwritten, but neither the executive, the legislature, nor the judiciary has any more power than that granted to it by the constitution. Democracy then functions within the limits set by the constitution or the law.

Democracy as process. Viewed as process, democracy is a means or a system for getting at decisions and for taking group action. It is much broader in its implications than simply providing a formal framework by which certain representatives of the people are selected by the people to carry on the public work and are then held accountable to the people at the time of the next election. This is part of a democratic process in a representative republic or democracy. But in its deeper meanings, democracy as a process is at work in all situations in which groups of free and intelligent human beings must make decisions and arrive at courses of action.

Democratic process is not a way of arriving at speculative or theoretical truth. The philosopher in his study and the scientist in his laboratory are not engaged in democratic process. There the mind of the individual person is at work. Neither does democratic process apply to works of fine art in which the individual talent and feeling of the artist give meaning and beauty to the artistic creation. But it does apply to that whole spectrum of human activity in which human beings must act jointly and where decisions made by the group directly affect the lives of its members.

As process, democracy demands that all those who have a right to be heard should be heard before a decision is taken. It means that all available relevant information shall be brought to bear on the discussion. It requires that all participate: those who are well informed as well as those who are poorly informed, although all have the obligation to inform themselves as fully as possible. Democratic process implies an openness to ideas, a desire to learn from others, and a search for an answer that will be most acceptable to all. It requires, further, that all be willing to hear the evidence and the arguments, to communicate freely and honestly with one another, to compromise where possible, and to accept the responsibility for helping to make the final decision a rich and meaningful one. If, as is often the case, consensus is impossible, the democratic process calls for a majority vote. The majority decides which course of action is to be taken, and the decision is accepted by all as the most practicable solution. Democratic process provides clearly, however, for the protection of the rights of the minority, including the right to work to become the majority.

Democracy as process has been compared to the scientific method. The comparison is apt at several points but perhaps nowhere more so than at the point of final decision. Just as the scientific method does not ever claim to produce the sure or complete answer at any moment, neither does the democratic process. All that is claimed is that this is the best way of arriving at a decision or an answer at this time under these circumstances. All who are concerned have had a chance to help shape it. All are responsible for it, even those who most opposed it. Just as the scientist is well aware that a new hypothesis or additional information may turn up to change or even invalidate his conclusion, so, too, in the democratic process all are aware that the decision might have been different and that it might have to be changed in the light of new developments.

Considered either as content or as process, democracy is not inevitable. Those who say that democracy so corresponds with the nature of man and so fulfills the life of man and of society that all people will, sooner or later, come to see its advantages have no warrant in history for such a position. Democracy is both an experiment and an adventure; it cannot be taken for granted. Both those who love power and efficiency and those who have closed ideologies will find democracy intolerable. Democracy, like liberty, is won only at the price of eternal vigilance. Democracy is won, too, only by good and effective education.

Education Essential to the Establishing of Democracy

Democracy is based on the premise that man is free. He is neither an instrument nor a slave. He is an end, not a means. Unless man is free, democracy is meaningless.

But the freedom of man can be viewed in at least two ways. Man is free *ontologically*. He is free, as some hold, in a theological sense by reason of his existence as a child of God. Others would hold that he is indeed ontologically free, but in the metaphysical or philosophical sense that he possesses spiritual faculties of intellect and will which enable him to share in the free world of the spirit. As an intelligent being man can foresee ends and choose among the means to these ends. Man is free *operationally*. He is operationally free insofar as he becomes free, insofar as he actually lives a life of freedom. Ontological freedom is the ground and reason for operational freedom, but it is entirely possible for a man to be ontologically free and not operationally free. The prisoner in a concentration camp, for example, is ontologically free but not operationally so.

This section is concerned only with man's operational freedom and it seeks to make the point that man becomes operationally free primarily through education. If democracy depends on, and demands, freedom, then education is essential to the establishment and preservation of democracy. Education is the means by which man becomes operationally free and thus capable of democracy.

One of the best definitions of education, perhaps somewhat over-simplified, is that it is a process of *liberation,* and liberation is the process by which one becomes free. One must, of course, acquire the tools of education—i.e., the symbols of language and of numbers, the interests, the aptitudes, and the discipline—before he can begin his education, but in the strict sense these are propaedeutic. Formal education begins in earnest when the student encounters what have long been called the *liberal* studies, the liberal arts and sciences, and normally this takes place well before he reaches college age.

Some historians of education contend the original concept of liberal education was that it was that type of education considered proper for the free man rather than for the slave. The free man was the ruler; the slave was compelled to obey. Whatever the original meaning, liberal education has come to mean that kind of education by means of which man becomes free. It is the education suitable for every man born to be free. Ontologically this means all men. In a democracy it also operationally means all men. If this is true, it follows logically that that type of education which is most essential to democracy is liberal education. Some prefer the term *general education* but there is no difference in meaning between the terms *general education* and *liberal education.*

Education and liberation. To liberate means, of course, *to make free.* Freedom, however, is not a neutral, passive, or indifferent condition, as if liberation meant nothing more than unlocking a door or removing a barrier. Freedom is not merely the absence of restraint or constraint; it is, rather, a positive sharing in the fully human life, the life of genuine culture and dignity. Freedom is possible only to spiritual beings—vegetables and brute animals, though living, are not free. Freedom consists of the exercise and perfection of man's spiritual powers. This is the sense of the Scripture which says: "You shall know the truth and the truth shall set you free."

But how does liberal education liberate man and help him to become free? Liberal education is that education which is proper to man as man; it has no specific purpose or reference other than to his liberation. It does not seek to make him rich, skillful, artistic, honored, or powerful, but only to make him wise and good. It seeks to make him more fully what he is: a man. It seeks to broaden and deepen his spiritual powers so that he can gain freedom through the quality of his life as a human being.

Liberal education. Like democracy itself, liberal education is both a content and a process. It is something to be taught as well as a particular way of teaching it.

Liberal education is concerned with acquainting each person with those things in life which are most true, most good, and most beautiful. It is likewise concerned with providing the standards by which one judges what is true, what is good, and what is beautiful. The content of liberal education is not to be found in any one set of books nor even in any one cultural tradition. Liberal education's content is never exhausted because it extends to the nature of God, the universe, man, and society.

Liberal education is also a process, a particular approach to those things which are to be studied and known. Liberal education takes place in what is called *the liberal mode.* It is this approach or mode which differentiates liberal education from the knowledge or education proper to the specialist. Liberal education seeks the inner spirit, life, meaning, beauty, and richness of that which is known, not the full-blown and profound knowledge of the specialist. The mode characteristic of liberal education produces the man of culture, of what the Greek civilization called *Paideia.*

Taught in this mode, the student comes to know the fundamental relationships, implications, and basic principles of a discipline. For example, history taught in the liberal mode is taught in such a way that the student will understand its cultural value even though he may never become an historian.

Liberal education is not superficial; it is just as profound as specialized education but it is directed by its own distinctive mode. A sound democracy requires that liberal or general education be widespread among its citizens.

Education "About" and "In" Democracy

In considering the role of education in the growth of a country or a culture toward democracy, it is necessary to suggest the two ways in which education both aids in that growth and makes it possible. Education is not just a catalyst in the process; it is one of the essential components. On the one hand, there is an important body of knowledge, information, or principles *about* democracy which must be learned through the educational process. On the other hand, there is a whole system of democratic practices, procedures, meanings—in short, the actual living of democracy—which comprises education *in* democracy. Both are essential; democracy can not work if either is missing. The one is theoretical; the other is practical. Education seeks to bring democratic practice into as close accord as possible with democratic theory.

Democracy is more than just a feeling, an attitude, or an approach to life. It is also a definite body of knowledge, though it is never a closed or completed system; its principles are firm but one of these very principles is that changing conditions will require changes in thinking. It is correct, for this reason, to speak of growth "toward" democracy. Democracy, like human freedom or Christian charity, is never fully realized though it may be achieved in varying degrees.

First of all, the theory of democracy is a complex and multi-faceted study, not an exact science. Democracy is not subject to quantification. It cannot be reduced to any formula. It cannot be readily validated by experimental verification of hypotheses. Yet it can be and must be known or learned in an organized and systematic way.

The study about democracy would have to start with the assumption that it is *something to be learned*. Whether it is regarded as a distinct subject matter or as a composite study to which teachers from many disciplines contribute would be a matter of choice. Several different approaches have already been tried. A course in elementary or secondary school or even college called simply *Democracy* can be a direct and realistic means of studying about democracy. It can also be a highly integrative course.

In studying about democracy one would analyze the theoretical principles on which it stands. Attention would be given to the history of democracy throughout the ages in an attempt to determine which environmental factors contribute to its success and which to its failures. The psychological laws and motivations which underlie democracy would be examined. The great literature on democracy would be read. The purpose of such a study would be to make sure that one knew democracy thoroughly by knowing about it. Although value judgments are implicit in all teaching and learning, the purpose of such a study would not be to indoctrinate.

Democracy is not, of course, simply a speculative matter. It is not something that one learns just for its truth content. Democracy is a very practical matter. It is a way of life, a way of doing things, which penetrates deeply every phase of life's practical affairs. Consequently, if democracy is to be effective, the citizens must learn not only about democracy in a speculative way; they must also learn democracy. There must be education *in* democracy.

What does this mean? Education in democracy means learning democracy by actually experiencing its functioning. It means actually being a party to, or a member of, the democratic process in operation. It means, though the grammatical expression seems strange: learning democracy by "doing" democracy. One cannot come to a genuine understanding of democracy or an appreciation of it, if he has not personally experienced it through participation.

The education system in a democracy, then, necessarily has as one of its responsibilities a program of education *in* democracy. Other agencies in society will also have occasion and opportunity to educate in democracy or democratic living, but the schools alone have the best opportunity to provide such education under supervision and at a time when impressions are most lasting. The schools can educate in democracy in a designed way. They have the time; they also have the techniques for evaluating and suggesting improvement. If education *in* democracy is, in part, the actual process of learning how to participate in group decisions, how to communicate well, how to share in planning, how to assume responsibility for decisions, where better can this be learned than in the school and classroom, in extracurricular activities as well as through the curriculum itself?

In a democracy, the schools have a primary function, just as does every other institution in society. The schools are rightly considered the home of theory, not the home of practice. Their first duty is intellectual formation and development, and with reference to democracy itself this would mean their first duty would be to teach *about* democracy. The schools should let nothing interfere with their primary function. But, in fact, they cannot help also educating *in* democracy.

It will be helpful to point out a few things that education in democracy is *not*. It is not a theory that all human concerns can be settled by vote. It is not simply a process of learning how to adjust and to make compromises. It is not a device for coming to treat everyone's ideas and opinions as of equal worth. It is not a matter of learning how to promote one's own interests, likes, and preferences. It is not a way of making friends or preserving peace at any price.

Education in democracy is, on the contrary, a realistic way of learning to live and work with people. It is learning that the best answers are not always the easiest or the fastest. It is an avenue of individual development through self-expression based on the fact that no one has all the answers and that, depending on circumstances, everyone has a right to be heard. It is learning to cooperate and participate, to assume the burdens of leadership as required and the responsibility for one's own decisions at all times. It is coming to realize that all people have equal rights but that not all people have equal ability. It is, in short, coming to realize practically that democracy, since democracy is people, has in it all the strength and weaknesses of all the people. Education in democracy is the best way of overcoming weaknesses and developing strengths.

Education and Legislation

There are those strong proponents of democratic theory who maintain that democracy can be achieved and made genuinely viable only by legislation. Those who desire a democratic mode of political life must seize political power and, in a sense, democratically enforce democracy. These proponents are thoroughly convinced of the democratic cause; they consider its development far too important to be left to the chance and uncertainty of education. They think of education as too slow-moving, as always in the process of catching up, as too closely tied to traditional and prevailing forms ever to bring about significant political and social changes.

They regard the power of the law, rather than education, as the great moving force toward democracy. In the same way, for them democracy is made strong through legal enactment, not through education.

This thinking is not without its theoretical and historical roots. A quick reading of history might even seem to confirm it. In point of fact, democracy has almost always come into existence before the people could be said to have been ready for it. But this point of view fails to take into account several important aspects of the relationship between education and legislation and of the relationship of both to democracy.

First of all, education, properly understood, is the source of those ideas which propel a nation toward democracy. Whether, historically, these ideas are perceived at first by only a small number of men is not at issue. New ideas are almost inevitably the work of a small number of men. But these creative men and their ideas are the product of many life forces, the most important of which is the education they have received. The founding fathers of the American republic, for example, were all very well-educated men. The ideas and the plan of government on which they eventually settled can easily be traced back in large part to the authors they had read and to the teachers under whose influence they had come. Similarly, for example, many of the men who have been most responsible for the establishment of democracies among the emerging countries of Africa are men who came to know democracy through their education and their experience in the leading universities of Europe and America.

Furthermore, legislation is essential to every society. But if it rests only on external coercion, it will disrupt society rather than serve it. The law, if the people who are subject to it have had no part in its formulation, is only as good as the enforcing power. It takes a good police force to make a bad or unpopular law work. People who do not approve of the law will act contrary to its spirit or they will openly rebel against it. Legislation to which the people must conform whether they like it or not is not in the democratic spirit. It is often necessary, however, in those countries in which rule is by *the one* or by *the few*.

Legislation which is not in keeping with the thinking of the people will be, at best, ineffective. It might be a threat to the stability of the society. Education has the twofold task of developing the understanding of the people to the point where they will see what legislation is necessary and good and also of helping to shape their attitudes and their thinking so that a minimum of legislation will be necessary. Though no one holds that any society could exist in the real order without legislation, it is correct to say that to the extent legislation is necessary, to that extent democracy has failed.

Thus, at any point in the development of democracy, education and legislation play complementary and mutually supporting roles. Legislation is also a form of education. On the other hand, education makes it possible for the people themselves, either directly or through their wisely selected representatives, to share in the actual process of legislating. In a democracy, legislation should be the legislation of the people. In general, education is more fundamental and more lasting than legislation and it is more in keeping with the democratic ideals of human freedom and human dignity.

Finally, though education may not have the same boldness and drama as legislation, it has the great value of building slowly and firmly and of establishing democracy on a sure basis. People can be legislated into doing things which are in their own best interests and those of society, but if they do not see their best interests lie in this legislation they will not cherish it even though they might obey it. A democracy based on legislation is still an immature democracy. With the deeper understandings which education affords, democracy can become richer in meaning and more permanent.

CHAPTER VI

Education Strengthened by Democracy

Education is a powerful and indispensable element in the growth of a country toward democracy. Democracy, once established, provides both the inspiration and environment for education to achieve its deepest and best purposes. Man's education, like man's spirit itself, cannot be pressed, shackled, and forced. It flourishes in some surroundings and not in others.

Dignity of the Individual

As has been seen, democracy springs from the profound realization that each individual person shares in essential human nature.[1] His human nature itself gives each man a valid claim to dignity and respect. However one accounts for and defines human nature, there is agreement among all men that human nature is radically and distinctively different from nonhuman forms of life. Some maintain it is a difference of *kind;* others, a difference of *degree.* All admit it is a vast difference. Society, too, has its proper and important claims to respect, but society exists finally for the good of the person and not vice versa. Within this general spirit and understanding, education can live and serve both the person and society.

Only in a society which recognizes the dignity of the individual can education have full and proper latitude in pursuing its purpose of assisting individuals to realize this dignity. For education, if it is to be anything more than indoctrination or training, is strictly an individual matter. All education is the education of the individual

---

[1] The idea of "the immutable nature of a thing"—here specifically the nature of a human being—is one of the most profound contributions of classical Greek philosophy to human thought. It is an irreducible metaphysical concept. It holds that the essences or natures of things do not change, although there will be wide accidental variations and changes among those sharing the same nature. In this thinking, neither education nor evolution affect man's essential nature.

Modern evolutionary theory, on the other hand, tends to deny the concept of essence or nature. In this theory all things change and the kinds and amounts of change are factors of time and circumstance.

person, though it takes place in society and is a social act. The principal efficient agent in all education is the student himself, not any outside force such as the teacher, the books, or the curriculum. Philosophers of education speak of the teacher as the instrumental cause of a student's coming to know. The teacher is a cooperative artist in that he cooperates with the student's natural learning power. The teacher can assist the student to learn, but he can neither learn for him nor force him to learn.

If genuine education could be externally imposed or induced, then it might flourish in a society in which the dignity of the individual was not understood or appreciated. But if education is rightly regarded as an inward matter, private, personal, individual, and never exactly the same for any two persons, then an understanding of the dignity of the individual is essential to it. Education takes place within the individual; it is proper and particular to him. Even identical or similar educational stimuli will not produce the same results in any two individuals. Thus, the real meaning, the effectiveness, and the dignity of education itself depend in an important way on the concept of the dignity of the individual.

Closely related to the awareness of the dignity of the individual, and an essential condition of education in a democracy, is a regard for individual differences. This regard is a powerful and pervasive quality of education in a democracy. Countries with other forms of rule may distinguish among individuals so that their special talents and capacities can be carefully assigned in the service of the State. But democracy places great emphasis on individual differences for the sake of the individual person himself and his highest fulfillment. In a democracy the individual makes his own choices; he is not assigned a place and a role in life.

So much stress is put on individual differences in the democratic theory of education that students of education are likely to regard the idea as perhaps even overworked. Critics of democratic theory in education sometimes fear that the emphasis on individual differences threatens the common and general learning necessary for unity in any society. Nonetheless, the accent on individual differences in education flows inevitably from democracy's fundamental insight concerning the dignity of the individual.

The concept of individual differences is not complicated. Empirical psychology confirms that there are vast differences among individual persons. For example, some persons are bright and others are relatively slow; some strong, others weak; some like to study or read, others prefer more active pursuits; some are highly emotional, others are unemotional; some are skilled at one thing, others at another. The range of differences on any one scale—the intelligence scale, for example—is great and, to some degree, measurable.

The fact that individuals differ greatly from one another does not mean that they do not also have much in common. As an example: persons living in the same country will ordinarily share a common language; they share a common history; they enjoy a common literature. Education in a democracy must contain important elements that are common to all. But at the same time democracy supports and urges an education based on the differences among individuals. Education is not standardized, regimented, and mechanized. Those who show exceptional intellectual ability receive a different education from those who do not. Democracy does not confront the youngster with the choice of either pursuing studies of which he is not capable or receiving no education at all. But at the same time democratic theory does not imply that there are to be no standards in education and that education is to be made so easy that anyone can get it.

Within the individual classroom, the teacher will seek to plan his instruction so that differences in ability, motivation, and preference, are not overlooked. Through the process called "sectioning" many schools and many classrooms are arranged in such a way as to provide for differences in ability and performance among students. Although it is not true to say that the instruction is child-centered in the sense that his interests become the exclusive guidelines, it is true to say that the child is regarded as an individual, important in himself, and not as a number or a vague, faceless figure.

Even in the most highly developed democracies, much remains to be done in taking individual differences into account in educational planning. Shortages of money and personnel and problems of administration are likely always to be obstacles to programming for individual differences. But in a democracy the spirit and the understanding are there. Democratic theory stands in complete unity with educational theory on this issue.

Equal Opportunity

The democratic principle of equal opportunity, again, rests squarely on the proposition that all men share equally in essential human nature. If they did not, the principle of equal opportunity would be either meaningless or sentimental. No man is "more" of a man than any other. Each man fulfills the definition of man as much as any other. If this is true, then each person should have the same opportunity to fulfill himself as an individual. A man is not "less" a man or "more" a man because the color of his skin happens to be white, black, brown, or red. There is no proof that some men are innately or natively more intelligent or more capable of love than others.

The doctrine of equality includes only essentials; it does not apply to the accidental aspects or qualities of human existence. All men are equal before the law and all are entitled to equal treatment under the law. It is literally true that all men are created equal. Human beings, however, differ vastly in specific qualities—learning ability, energy, attitudes, and preferences. These differences will be found within any group or society. Important as these differences may be in the course of human development, they are only accidental differences among men. Singly or cumulatively, they never make an essential difference in human nature.

A democratic society steeped in belief in human equality and in the practice of equal opportunity which human equality implies creates the climate in which education can function to maximum advantage. What does *equal opportunity* in a democracy mean? In general, it means that no person shall be denied the chance to share in the present or potential good of the society by reason of his race, his religion, his class, or his nationality. All citizens will be given the same access to opportunities and advantages. Some citizens will not be arbitrarily privileged and others deprived. Improvement and advancement are not closed to any citizen by socially imposed conditions over which he has no control. Society itself does not predetermine who will move ahead, who will have a chance to express and fulfill himself, and who will be the leaders and who the led. The doctrine of equal opportunity does not assure anyone of equal success, but it assumes that everyone will have an equal chance for success.

In the context of the relationship between democracy and education, equal opportunity has two broad aspects: (1) equal opportunity and education itself; (2) equal opportunity in the life of the democracy.

Equal opportunity and education. The concept of equal opportunity applies both to the opportunity to undertake the educational effort in the first place and to reasonable equality of treatment within the educational system.[2] It is a generalized concept and it means as well that educational opportunity will keep pace with the changing conditions in a man's life. Educational opportunity is not a specific chance which, once lost, is lost forever.

The general doctrine of equal opportunity in a democracy applies, of course, to equality of educational opportunity. But in this application the doctrine is widely misunderstood; it requires special analysis.

The concept of equal educational opportunity is especially subtle because education is the very process through which youngsters prove they are unequal in so many different ways. It would be a complete misreading of the doctrine of equality for a democracy to strive to give an identical education to all youngsters. It must strive, however, to give each youngster an equal opportunity to gain an education appropriate to his own interests and abilities. Even if it were possible to provide an identical education for all, such an education would be meaningless to some, unfair to many, and, in a sense, undemocratic for all. Equal opportunity cannot and does not mean identical educational programming. The one place in which youngsters cannot be treated as identical is in the matter of education. Equal educational opportunity implies that each will have a good chance to show what he can do and will do. Rapid learners, for example, will not get an education identical to that of slower learners, but all students will have the opportunity to show whether they are bright or slow and they will have an equal opportunity to

---

2 "In the time of Solon and Cleisthenes, the fathers of their democracy, the Athenians did not believe that democracy meant license, that freedom meant anarchy, that equality under the law meant freedom to say anything one wished, and that the highest happiness was the power to do what one wanted without hindrance: instead, by punishing men of that type, the state tried to make its citizens better. The equality they strove to achieve was not mechanical equality which gave each man what was due to him." Werner Jaeger, *Paideia: The Ideals of Greek Culture*, Vol. III: *The Conflict of Cultural Ideals in the Age of Plato* (New York: Oxford University Press, 1943), p. 113. Translated by Gilbert Highet.

improve and advance to their fullest capacity. Schools will be provided for all and not just for some, and a democracy will seek to make sure that the quality of education within the school is as good for all as it is for some.

Furthermore, equal educational opportunity does not imply that it is the *same* opportunity. In a democracy all youngsters will not have the same opportunity but they will have equal educational opportunities. For this reason, some theorists prefer to speak of *equity* of opportunity rather than of *equality* of educational opportunity. By this they mean that each youngster in a democracy will have a fair or just share in that democracy's educational opportunities. Provision will be made to insure that the educational opportunities are equitably or justly distributed. Other theorists, however, maintain that equity of opportunity and equality of opportunity really amount to the same thing. If it is understood that *equal to* does not mean *identical with,* then opportunities are equitable only if they are equal. In this sense, to give each individual his due (equity) means precisely to give each one an equal opportunity. An equal opportunity is each man's due in a democratic society.

A further analysis of the word *opportunity* might be helpful. The word derives from two Latin words, *ob* and *portum,* meaning *to* or *toward a port.* Its usage was originally nautical. By it sailors indicated that certain winds were favorable or opportune in that they carried the ship toward shore or port. Etymologically, then, an opportunity is a "favorable wind." It is not just the absence of impediment or interference; rather, it is a positive and favorable assistance which helps to bear or carry one toward his port or goal.

Educational opportunity, in the same way, is not just the absence of restriction. It is the positive setting of the conditions which will be favorable and conducive for one's receiving an education appropriate for him and in the best interests of society. In a democracy this opportunity should become, insofar as possible, equal for all.

Democracy seeks to make it possible for all youngsters in the society to gain an education. Those who have poor parents as well as those who have rich parents will be able to go to school and to advance in the educational system as far as their talents will permit. The ideal is that no person in a democracy will ever be able to say that he did not have a chance or that he was the victim of unfair discrimination.

No youngster will be barred from the schools because he does not dress well enough, because he does not have the "right" color skin, or even because he does not speak the "right" language. Equal opportunity seems to imply that education shall be made available to all on a free or publicly supported basis, though the strict reading of the doctrine does not require that education should be compulsory. The idea of equal opportunity in education does not necessarily suggest that all shall be forced by law to take advantage of the opportunity. Education—good education—will be made accessible to all.

Equal opportunity in education implies, too, that all youngsters will receive the same general treatment within the school system. It does not suggest that all will receive the same type of education but only that the differentiations will be based on educational considerations—not on such extraneous reasons as color, race, or creed. It implies that all youngsters will be given the opportunity to discover their talents and to develop them. It means that whatever advantages are open to some will be, insofar as possible, open to all providing only that they qualify. It means that other types of education will be made available to those who cannot benefit from or who are not interested in the traditional types and forms of education.

It can also be argued that the doctrine of equal opportunity in education carries with it the obligation of society to make it not only possible but also relatively convenient for all to get an education. Equality of educational opportunity implies being able to take advantage of the opportunity. Every society is limited in what it can do and what it should do to provide equal educational opportunity, but whatever it can and should do, it should do for all.

Equal opportunity in the life of democracy.   In a democracy, the doctrine of equal opportunity applies not only in education but also in the general life of the culture or country. No one will be prevented from being President of the country or a successful professional or business man because he lacked the opportunity. Every man will have an equal opportunity to vote and to express himself. Above all, he will have the opportunity to make his own opportunities.

Equal opportunity in education and in life is, of course, a source of strength in a democracy. It makes it possible for the democracy to take full advantage of the various talents of each and all of its citizens. Those who have ability have the chance to show it and prove it. The vast reserve of talent that remains untapped in some countries because it never has a chance to develop is released in a democracy. People have the possibility of doing what they want to do and like to do and consequently have the chance of excelling at it. If only a few have the opportunity for an education, only those few will have the ideas and the training necessary for the functioning of society and for sharing in its culture.

Equal opportunity in the general life of the democracy is also a powerful incentive for youngsters to gain an education and make the most of it. Those who realize that their education will determine how far they will be able to advance in society and how much they will be able to contribute to it will work diligently to succeed in it. They will see that education is meaningful both for their own fulfillment and for the good of society. The fact that democratic society is open and affords equal opportunity to all gives vitality and significance to education. Those who get an education will have genuine opportunity to benefit themselves and others by means of it. Their ideas will be listened to, their voting will be more mature and more meaningful, their special and unique talents will be appreciated.

Freedom of Inquiry

The freedom to inquire is a fundamental right of the democratic charter that directly relates to education and greatly strengthens it. Inquiry is, of course, the process of exploring, analyzing, pursuing information, asking questions, and seeking answers. Its value resides in the fact that it makes it possible for a person to arrive at free and independent judgments so that he can act on principles as he sees them and on firm conviction. Inquiry is not an end in itself; it is a means of arriving at one's own conclusions. To inquire is part of the act of thinking and in a democracy one is free to, and forced to, think for himself rather than have someone else dictate his thoughts for him and to him.

Freedom of inquiry implies that no areas of human knowledge are beyond inquiry or further investigation. No belief, no prejudice, no conclusion is so rigid that it is regarded as settled once and for all. Each form of knowledge, each methodology, each idea must remain open to further scrutiny. It must be able to stand the test put to it by subsequent developments, by further or deeper information, and by improved techniques of investigation. Ideas are neither accepted nor rejected by fiat.

Freedom of inquiry implies, further, that the means of inquiry be available. Education itself is the major means. There will be full and free access to information. Neither books, teachers, nor ideas will be dismissed simply on the grounds that they run contrary to accepted or prevailing positions. No part of the inquiry is arbitrarily forestalled because the conclusions might be thought to be harmful to certain interests. Essential, also, is the fact that the channels of communications be left open and that no iron curtain be rung down around certain areas of inquiry by religious, political, academic, or social authorities or power groups. Freedom of inquiry is a necessary derivative and corollary of the rational nature of man. Without it, genuine education is impossible.

Academic freedom is, in turn, a corollary of the right to inquire. It, too, is an important aspect of democratic life and a further way that democracy strengthens the educative effort. Academic freedom is best considered as the fulfillment of the right to inquire, and as a special phase of the freedom of expression. In a democratic society a man has the right and, where appropriate, the obligation to share the fruit of his inquiry. Academic freedom means that any qualified scholar who has undertaken the process of inquiry with intellectual honesty, and who has merited the privilege of teaching because he has become learned, has the right to teach in accordance with his own findings. He is not to be held accountable to some authority presumably higher than the scholarly and intellectual process itself. Academic freedom is democracy's way of safeguarding itself against those forces which, in every society, seek to control thought and inquiry.

Without the freedom to inquire, education becomes so enfeebled that it soon ceases to be education at all. The students and even the teachers are required to accept blindly, passively, and uncritically what has been laid down or told them by others. Education thus loses both its vitality and its honesty. Socrates said: "The unexamined life is not worth living." In a similar vein, education is not worth pursuing if there is no real freedom to inquire and examine.

Only when freedom of inquiry is not only permitted but encouraged does education become an active, probing, and exciting process. The minds of the students are challenged rather than prematurely closed. Students are asked to take a second look, to insist on explanations, to speculate and conjecture about alternatives, to propose new possibilities, to test results. Students are required to do their own thinking even though they realize that an essential part of the process of inquiry is to study attentively what the great thinkers, both past and present, have thought and said on the matter. Inquiry is essential both to confirm one's present thinking and to change it.

Self-Criticism and Evaluation

Another of the great strengths of education in a democracy is the very openness of that democracy to self-criticism and self-evaluation. Both of these important aspects of democratic life lend strength and vitality to the educational process at every level. The word *criticism*, as it is used here, has a Greek origin and it means *the ability to discuss, judge,* and *discern.*

Criticism does not at all imply hostility or antagonism toward democracy. Self-criticism means that those living within the system and maintaining friendly attitudes toward it can nevertheless determine freely whether the theory and ideals of democracy are being applied and practiced as well as they might. Self-criticism is neither narcissistic nor radically revolutionary. Democracy is best understood by those who live within it and it does not wait to be judged by those outside who do not know its meaning or its spirit. Criticism seeks not to destroy democracy but to improve it. Freedom to criticize is based on the profoundly optimistic premise that democracy is fundamentally right and good and that it will not only survive, but will also advance in an environment which welcomes criticism. It is also based on the realistic premise that very little, if anything (including democracy), is ever perfect.

Criticism and evaluations are, to be sure, closely related concepts. They are differentiated here because criticism implies an active and alert—perhaps even a formal—effort to point out strengths and weaknesses. Evaluation as part of the ordinary exercise of intelligence need not be so formal or intentional.

As will be seen later, one of the great problems in a democracy is to determine the criterion or criteria according to which valid criticisms or evaluations can be made. For the moment, it is necessary only to point out that criticism and evaluation within a democracy do not draw their standards or criteria from outside the process. For example, democracy does not accept, as does modern Communism, the writings of Marx or Lenin, Stalin or Khrushchev, as the final authority on whether an idea, an institution, or a movement is good or bad. In Communist theory, criticism and evaluation, when permitted at all, stop at the point of determining whether an idea or a practice is in conformity with what Marx and Lenin have written. No deviation from the Party line is permitted. If the idea or practice does not conform, it is disallowed *a priori*. In democratic theory, an idea or a practice is evaluated on the basis of its own merits. It is given as fair, as impartial, and as objective a hearing as possible.

Both criticism and evaluation are essential aspects of democratic theory. Progress is impossible without them. They are not appendages to it or afterthoughts. All persons who will be affected by a decision are expected and urged to take a critical look at whatever is being proposed and they are urged to seek ways of evaluating the proposal. It is both contrary to the democratic spirit and irresponsible to accept an idea simply because someone else has accepted it. It is equally irresponsible to reject an idea out of hand without carefully criticizing it and evaluating it.

Why are the practices of criticism and evaluation such great strengths of education in a democracy? Most simply, because they make it possible for education to carry out fully its true and proper function. Criticism and evaluation are as important to education as they are to democracy. It might also be said that they are important to any fully rational and completely human life. The role of reason is to point out strengths and weaknesses in every phase of life and to evaluate how well or how successfully the intended purposes are being achieved. This, too, is the most profound significance of education—to make it possible for man to live more humanly and more humanely.

Education, properly conceived, seeks to equip a person with the understanding, the knowledge and information, the sensitivity, and the keenness of mind and intellect he will need to criticize and to evaluate well. The school curriculum aims at supplying in the clearest possible way the tools and the language, the necessary background information, and the principles and concepts on which valid and constructive criticism and evaluation can be based. The schooling or formal educational process also seeks to supply the desire and the habit of criticism or critical thinking. Whether it is in literature or history, in the social or the natural sciences, in philosophy or theology, the good teacher will assist his students to make comparisons, to analyze, to examine other possibilities, to find relationships and disparities, to probe beneath the obvious, to question the obscure.

Democracy thus lends both its spirit and its deepest meaning to education which takes place within it. One supports and reinforces the other and both benefit greatly. Education cannot be true to itself and democracy cannot long exist without intelligent criticism and evaluation.

Creativity and Change

A democratic society is necessarily an open and free society. It might be called a restless society, for the dynamics of change are essentially built into it. The emphasis in a democracy is always much more on the future than on the past, although this does not imply that the past is neglected or dishonored in any way. A democratic society is not a stable and rigid society. It is open to change and it places high value on creative thinking. The only sure test of an idea is how it survives the competition of rival ideas which are freely studied and freely presented. Neither forms nor processes are irrevocably pre-established. Tensions and pressures are a sign of life and are integral to democratic society for it is a society made strong by life and movement.

Sound educational theory holds that learning takes place best when it is active and meaningful—i.e., when the student puts not only his efforts but also his values into it. If the student realizes his own thinking is important and will make a difference, he will engage more fully in the learning process. If the society welcomes rather than resents or fears new ideas, schooling becomes more than a routine and mechanical process. It becomes a profound means of self-expression and self-fulfillment and an active and exciting encounter.

To encourage creativity or creative thinking is, also, an important function of education. In a democracy this function of education can be most significantly achieved.

What is the meaning and value of creative thinking? Creative thinking takes place at many levels and in many ways. It is that type of thinking which results in perceiving new relationships between ideas, between theories and practices, between structure and process, and among past and present and future. Creative thinking leads, naturally enough, to new ways of looking at things and new ways of doing things. It brings about refinements in techniques and in standards. It discovers new resources and seeks out better ways of using old resources. It points the way to new and different meanings in religion, art, science, and technology. It seeks new solutions to age-old social, economic, and political problems.

In one sense, all genuine thinking is creative thinking. There is no such thing as noncreative thinking, although much that passes for thinking is noncreative in that it is a passive absorption or acceptance of knowledge and ideas. The student who does not question, who feels that his purpose is simply to master what is already known in the way it is already known, will never be a creative thinker. But the term *creative thinking* also has a fairly precise meaning which differentiates it from purely logical or discursive thinking. It implies an effort to see things in new or unusual combinations, to venture into untried areas, to make bold and intuitive leaps of the imagination, and to follow up even the faintest clues or the slightest discordancies. It reaches out to the unproven and the uncertain.

Psychologists have long been interested in the question of whether the ability to think creatively is mostly a factor of general intelligence or of environment. It is a matter of common observation that this ability exists in widely differing degrees within the same environment and that it also varies greatly from one environment to the other. Certain students, for example, will show much more capacity for creative thinking than others. In a democracy, education is quick to recognize creative ability among those students who possess it and to make provision for its development and expression. In a traditional, stable, and authoritarian society, there will be little creative thinking—and that only in limited and carefully circumscribed areas.

The point is simply that a democratic society is the most conducive political environment for creative thinking. The environment is responsive to new ideas; it rewards them highly if successful and it treats them gently and with respect even if they ultimately prove fruitless. The educational system serves both to create this environment and to strengthen it. And, in turn, this environment makes it possible for education to help its students achieve and exercise their capacities for creative thinking.

Creative thinking has a twofold value clearly recognized in a democracy. It is an important aspect of individual and personal human fulfillment. The person who thinks creatively shares most fully in the delights and challenges of human existence. His is a rich, deep, and rewarding life. He offers something of himself and he adds whatever he creates to the total accomplishment of the human race. Creative thinking is a great asset in the improving of life in society and in the solving of the social problems that beset every society. It has great value in the practical order. Creative thinking in the law and in legislation, in the arts and sciences, in business and technology, in social work and in services of all kinds, in military preparedness, and in international negotiations and international organization adds new solutions to current problems and helps to prevent problems from arising in the future.

Democracy is characterized by change—rapid, far-reaching change. Creative thinking inevitably leads to changes in ideas as well as in forms and patterns of living. Not all changes are for the better, and it would be most imprudent to assume that improvement in society takes place in a steady and straight line of progression. But change itself in a democracy and a generalized willingness to change do imply mobility and hope. This is a vast strength of education in a democracy because it suggests that each student must prepare himself well since he does not now know what the future will be for him. His motivation can be strong because his hopes and opportunities for the future can be strong. He can dream and he can succeed.

Education must seek to prepare the youngsters and students of today to live in a world in which things will be constantly changing. An education geared toward present facts, programs, and immediate applications might well leave the student unable to cope with the changing and changed conditions of a relatively few years from now.

It is a thorough grasp of the underlying principles and basic theories in every field of knowledge that makes it possible to foresee the directions change will take, to understand and master changes as they take place and, more important, to contribute one's best thinking in helping to control the very nature of the change itself.

CHAPTER VII

Problems of Education in a Democracy

Democracy, as a form of political organization, offers the best present hope and promise for a sound, vital, and significant educational system. Democracy makes it possible for education to function properly and education, in turn, serves well the purposes of democratic life. There is close and orderly correlation: if one succeeds, so does the other; if one fails, the other becomes ineffective.

This is not to say, however, that education in a democracy does not face serious and profound problems. Some of these problems are of a theoretical nature, touching on the very heart of the relationship between education and democracy. Others are of a more or less practical nature and can be attributed either to the shortcomings in the status of modern democracy or to the shortcomings of education. As the principles and processes of democracy become more widely and surely held, many of the latter problems will disappear. An example might well be the problem of racial integration in the schools. This problem in America, at least, and in other countries as well, arises not because of any defect in democratic theory but because of certain defects in the application of the theory.

It will be well to consider, however, some of the more fundamental problems of education in a democracy.

The Integrity of Education

Because democracy relies so heavily on education, there is the constant danger that education will come to be regarded as a means or an instrument for advancing the democracy. Good education will, to be sure, strengthen democracy and give it deeper meaning and fuller life. But it does this best by being true to its own principles. Education loses its integrity whenever it is used exclusively, or even primarily, as a means toward something else.

The temptation to think of education as a means rather than as an end is, of course, much less acute and obvious in a country ruled by *the many* than it is in a country ruled by *the one* or *the few*. Democratic theory itself contains safeguards against this view of education; other forms of rule and government tend to operate on the assumption that education is, indeed, a means toward political ends. In its very openness, democratic theory permits and almost forces an attempt to be independent and objective in judgment. Nonetheless, it is extremely important that both educators and laymen in a democracy understand what is meant by the *integrity of education*.

The term *integrity of education* implies that education, like knowledge, is an end in itself. It is not rightly to be considered as a means of supporting or validating some system. The principles which apply to education are proper principles and, like all genuine principles, they apply to education everywhere and at all times. Education is distorted, if not destroyed, by subservience to any system. Education has an integrity—a wholeness—of its own, just as it has a life of its own. It exists in a particular moment of history, a particular society and culture, but it derives its basic meaning from the character, the nature, and the essential needs and potentialities of man.

Theorists of education, writing from a democratic viewpoint, generally agree that education has its own integrity. Education is not an instrument for furthering particular causes or systems. It is not to be used for some ulterior end. Few theorists would disagree, for example, with the statement that education seeks to develop in youngsters and adults those habits by which they pursue that which is true, good, and beautiful.

But there is wide disagreement among theorists on the question of how to account for the integrity of education. Some maintain that education is a social institution, a creation of society, and that it gains its integrity by reason of a social consensus. Others maintain that education is the psychological response of a highly developed neuromechanism to the problems and difficulties of human existence. The integrity of education results from a widespread understanding among men of the best and most successful attempts to cope with these problems. The more commonly accepted metaphysical view is that education derives its integrity, its meaning, and its principles from an analysis of man and his nature. Man's happiness and fulfillment consists in knowing the true, in pursuing the good, and in appreciating the beautiful. The education of man must be integral if man himself is to be fulfilled and perfected as man.

The danger, of course, even in a democracy is that if the integrity of education is not understood and preserved, education will pursue ends or goals that are dictated by those who happen to be in power. It will make the soft and easy choices rather than the tough and necessary ones. It will follow the popular paths rather than the more difficult and demanding ones. Education will come more to adapt and serve than to set the standards and lead the way.

Public and Private Education

Democratic theory, as such, is neutral or impartial on the question of whether education in a democracy should be carried on under public or private auspices. Democracy cannot exist, let alone be strong, without a strong educational system, and the democratic State has both a right and an obligation to insist on certain educational standards. But the history of democracy reveals what is also clear from the theoretical analysis of democracy: that the educational process can be operated and conducted, with equal effectiveness, by either public or private authority.

Education in ancient Athenian democracy was in the hands of private tutors and pedagogues, and the development of education in Western civilization was, until the nineteenth century, largely in the hands of the Church or of private individuals. It is interesting to note, however, that education in the Orient—for example, in ancient China (although China was not in any sense of the word a democracy)—was controlled by the State from earliest times. In the West, the idea of education paid for out of public taxes and conducted under public auspices is a relatively recent innovation.

There is no question of the public character of education. Whether carried on under public or private auspices, education itself is always, at least in part, a public function and a public service in the public interest. Genuine education is never exclusively a private matter, just as human life is never exclusively personal or private. The quality of civil, social, and public life is dependent on the quality of education. As publicly controlled education came into the ascendancy, the question of whether education conducted under private auspices could serve the public interest as well as education conducted under public auspices inevitably arose.

Those who think that all education should be under direct public control and financed by public money maintain that a separate system of private schools tends to undermine the unity essential to democracy. They hold that private schools are divisive in that they emphasize the different rather than the common elements in society—differences based on conflicting religious, social, economic, political, or educational ideas. Private schools, it is held, have a private purpose to which the public purpose of education might well become subordinate.

On the other hand, those who see an important role for private education in a democracy feel it serves many purposes and has many good reasons. This feeling does not imply any lack of interest in, or regard for, public education. Rather, it is based on the idea that private education, by its very nature, can do certain things that would not be possible in a completely public educational system in a pluralistic society. Private education, so the argument runs, can perform all the essential educational tasks of the public schools and at the same time fulfill the special purposes for which it is designed. Furthermore, these theorists maintain, private education, far from being a threat to democracy, is one of its greatest strengths and assets. It provides the kind of diversity which does not disrupt unity, but, by distinguishing between unity and uniformity, fulfills it and gives it meaning.

The practical right of the private schools to exist, at least in the United States, has been clearly established by the decision of the Supreme Court of the United States in the famous Oregon School Case of 1925. Since the Supreme Court decided for the school sisters in the Oregon School Case, there have been no efforts in this country to disallow private schools by law, though the debate between the proponents of the public and private schools still continues. Sometimes it takes the form of theoretical discussions about the purposes of the school systems; at other times it takes the form of comparing the educational quality and effectiveness in the public and private schools.

The decision in the Oregon School Case was based on a fundamental principle of democratic theory: the primary rights in the education of their children belong to the parents. No claim of the

State and no theory of the importance of the common good can supercede the rights of the parents.

In loco parentis. The principle which is at the heart of the discussion of public and private education in a democracy is the principle that the primary right and responsibility for a child's education rests with his parents. The State may not interfere with this essential and sacred right, since it is, even in the natural order, a direct correlative of the fact of procreation. This is equivalent to saying that he who gives life to the body also gives life to the mind, the soul, and the spirit. The parents are not simply instruments or means for bringing children into the world, there to be turned over to the State. In a direct and literal and full way, parents can say that their children are *theirs,* not children of the State.

The State may and does, in the interest of the public welfare, insist that children be educated. It has secondary rights and interests in the education of its present and future citizens. It has the right of supervision and the right to enforce certain common standards and even certain common learnings. But to say that the State rightfully insists that youngsters be educated is far different from saying that the State can dictate how they are to be educated. This is an inalienable prerogative of the parents.

It is the right of the parents to determine whether their youngsters will attend public or private schools and, in turn, which among the many kinds of private schools they will attend.

The parents, however, may delegate their right and their authority to educate their youngsters to others. Ordinarily parents do not have the time, the background, or the formal means of education necessary to educate their youngsters themselves. This is especially the case in an advanced and complex society in which knowledge and training play such key roles. But the delegation of the authority to educate is to be decided by the parents themselves, not by the State. If the parent wants his youngsters to be educated in a private school he has every right to have them educated in that way.

Hence arises the principle that teachers and educators stand in the same relation to pupils and students as their own parents do. The teacher acts in the place of the parent. He is quite literally *in loco parentis,* whether in public or in private schools. The principle that the teacher takes over part of the educational task of the parent has two aspects: one, juridical; the other, operational.

Juridical.   The basis of the principle, *in loco parentis,* is the Roman law and English common law principle of agency.

In the legal or juridical order, the parent delegates his teaching authority to the school or the teacher by the very fact that he sends his youngster to him to be educated. In modern times this delegation does not involve a formal or written contract, though in the days when the apprenticeship program of education prevailed, it often did. The parent need not even be aware of the juridical implications of the fact that the teacher is acting in his name and as his agent.

But in every case of parent-to-teacher delegation of authority there is an implied contract. The parent has every right to assume that the teacher will act always in the best interests of the pupil or student. He has the right to assume that the teacher is in every way qualified to carry on the function of teaching. The parent literally contracts for the services of the teacher even though in modern societies the nature and terms of the contract are handled through regular formal administrative procedures often quite removed in time and space from the parent himself.

Operational.   According to the legal principles of agency, the agent's powers to act come from the principal and these powers can be as broad or as restrictive as the principal chooses to make them. In the actual order of operation in a democracy, the parent, as the principal, confers broad powers on his agent, the teacher. So much is this the case that the parent ordinarily leaves it to the teacher to use his own judgment and discretion in all matters pertaining to the pupil's education. The parent confers on the teacher, within the broadest possible limits, the right to act according to his own best thinking whether or not he as parent would have acted in the same way under similar circumstances. The proposed agent, the teacher, can refuse to accept the agency contract if he prefers to do so. Likewise, although he acts as the agent of the parent, the teacher also acts to some degree in his own name in accordance with the demands, duties, and prerogatives proper to the teaching profession. Both the parent and the teacher have appropriate legal recourse open to them if the cooperative effort fails and the implied contract breaks down.

The Financial Problem

Whatever the theoretical considerations, the realistic problem of finance is also basic to every analysis of public and private education in a democracy. It is now a clearly established principle that public authorities have the power to tax all the citizens in order to secure money to maintain and operate the public schools. This principle is of relatively recent vintage even in the United States (the Kalamazoo Case). The power to tax must be exercised in keeping with the established rules of democratic process. But it is now a principle to which no serious person in the democratic world objects.

As a result of the power to tax, the public school authorities have, for their educational use, whatever amount of money the affluence of the society and the interest of the citizens make possible. The financial situation of the private schools varies greatly from country to country. In some democratic countries (e.g., England) the private schools share on a proportionate basis in the monies collected through public taxes for educational purposes. In some countries (e.g., Canada) those parents who desire to send their youngsters to private schools receive a tax credit equivalent to the tuitions and fees at the private schools. In still other countries (e.g., the United States) those who send their youngsters to private schools must carry the entire financial burden of the private schools while at the same time they pay their full share of taxes for public educational purposes.

What is to be said of the financial position of the private schools in the United States? Private schools in this country are of two general types: those with a religious orientation or affiliation, and those which are strictly independent. The prevailing policy is that private schools of either type are not eligible for public financial assistance. This policy has a long history of popular approval; it has been confirmed by the nation's highest court. As is proper in a democracy, however, the policy has come up for almost constant review and re-examination.

The present policy is based on two considerations, one of which applies only to those private schools under religious sponsorship. The first consideration is that attendance at a private school is to be regarded as a privilege. Those who want to exercise this privilege must be willing to pay for it. The second consideration is that any subsidy from public funds for religious schools would constitute a violation of the constitutional principle of the separation of Church and State.

Those who hold that the present policy should be maintained advance several reasons for their position. The most cogent would seem to be: (1) Generally, private education, like any other private enterprise, should be supported by private funds. If sufficient funds are not available, the private school should go out of business. (2) The private school, without public financial assistance, is free, within limits, to operate in its own way. This might not be true if public control followed the public funds. (3) The principle of the separation of Church and State implies that public financial assistance to a religiously oriented school would in effect promote that particular religion. (4) Public support of private schools might endanger the public school system in that many more private schools of both types would be opened.

Those who hold that the present policy might well be changed also advance several significant arguments: (1) The private schools serve an important purpose in American society and they perform an educational function which promotes the public interest and public welfare in a way that ought to be encouraged rather than discouraged. (2) Ways could well be worked out, as they have been in other countries, of offering public financial assistance to private schools without in any way changing the private character of their administration and operation. (3) If parents have the right to send their youngsters to private schools, and if attendance at school is compulsory, the attending of private schools should not be considered a privilege but rather a simple matter of choice. (4) The principle of the separation of Church and State does not suggest that the government should be indifferent to, or hostile toward, religion, but only that it should not favor or promote any one religion over the others. Not all jurists agree by any means that public financial assistance to religious schools would violate the principle of the separation of Church and State. All religiously sponsored schools would be equally eligible for such public assistance.

The proponents of either side in this dispute do not line up necessarily along party lines. Many educators connected with the private schools would prefer that the policy remain as it is. In turn, many educators connected with the public school system, with an interest in strengthening all of American education, favor the granting of public financial assistance to the private schools.

The crux of the matter, however, is this: to be strong, education needs strong financial support. It is vital to the welfare of society that both public and private education be as strong as possible. The quality of education is not directly correlative to the amount of money spent on education, although this is one central index. Good education can take place wherever inspired teachers enter into contact with eager and attentive students. But it can be much better education when the facilities, the equipment, and the atmosphere are most conducive to the learning process, when the teachers have time and training for careful planning and follow-through, and when the ratio of students to teachers allows an opportunity for each student to have some of the teacher's personal attention. This is as costly as it is important.

The society that provides public financial support for public schools and leaves the support of private schools to doubly-taxed private individuals puts the private schools at a serious financial disadvantage. So great is this disadvantage that such a society runs the danger of losing its private schools altogether or of enduring a system in which large numbers of students do not get the best possible education.

Thought and Action

Another problem faced by education in a democracy is the fundamental question of the relationship of thought and action. The problem is simply stated, although in the context of the present study it takes many forms. Education traditionally—and, according to some theorists, rightfully—is concerned with thought and knowledge, with ideas, with the speculative and descriptive, with the forming of the mind or the intellect. Democracy, on the other hand, is centrally concerned with action, with solving practical rather than theoretical problems, and with getting things done. Education is oriented toward understanding; democratic process toward accomplishing and achieving.

In the process of getting things done democratically, each vote is as important as every other vote. The vote of the man who neither has good ideas of his own nor understands the good ideas of others is just as important in deciding on a course of action as is the vote of the man of broad and deep knowledge. Similarly, in the democratic process, there is danger that persuasion and rhetoric will replace logic and that compromise will replace conviction. Democratic process has the great advantage that whatever action is finally taken will have the support of, at least, the majority, but it runs the constant risk of missing the good idea for the acceptable one or the one that will win the most votes. The heroes of democratic society are not necessarily the men who think and most often they are the men who get things done.

Is democratic education anti-intellectual? Some theorists feel that a democratic society is virtually incapable of producing an objectively first-rate educational system. They maintain that education in a democracy is inevitably anti-intellectual. Not all of these theorists are opponents of democratic theory; some in fact regard democracy so highly that they are willing to sacrifice something of educational quality in order to preserve its deep-seated values and virtues. Their reasons for considering that education in a democracy will always be inferior are two:

1. To be effective in a democracy, ideas must capture the attention of the greatest number of people. The greatest number of people always fall in or below the middle range on any scale of intellectual ability. The vast majority of people will never be capable of understanding, or even interested in understanding, the great books, the great ideas, the great movements of history, the high moments of culture, for example, in science, music, art, or literature. Education tends to be carried on at the average level; it tends to become literally mass education. Even bright students do not want to appear bright, to be known as "eggheads," because this might seem to be undemocratic. Education in a democracy is doomed to mediocrity since the average man rules and is king, and since *the many* will always be average.

2. Education in a democracy is likely to be geared, perhaps even unconsciously, toward some kind of action: the usable or the salable. Education is most often thought of as a way of getting on in the world and of improving one's position. Its success is measured by what it does for one or what one does with it. Education is likely to be directed toward practical applications and to technology

rather than to basic research and abstract ideas. That knowledge is worth most which has the highest assignable value in the marketplace. In a democracy it is not sufficient to have an idea which will stand or fall depending on how competent people decide its merits; it is necessary also to be able to present that idea, in its most attractive light, to make it marketable, and to sell it.

The intellectual in democratic society.   Other theorists see the problem of the man of thought versus the man of action from a different point of view. They do not agree that democracy is inherently anti-intellectual. They see no essential reason why the work and the role of the intellectual should not be as highly respected in a democratic society as in any other. If, in the past, democracies have on occasion distrusted the intellectuals, it is not the fault of democratic theory but of the development of democracy. Far from thwarting or distorting thought, democratic process gives it fullest range and fullest freedom. The educational system seeks to provide opportunity for all, including those with exceptional intellectual abilities, to achieve an education which is limited only by individual interest and talent. If the educational system does not pay sufficient attention to thought and theory, this is a problem for education, but it does not result from democratic theory.

Furthermore, the intellectual has both a special responsibility to society and a profound contribution to make to it. He can and should lead the way for society in scholarship and research, in creating and in criticizing, and he can do this without in any way betraying the integrity of his calling. He may or may not have the time or the inclination to engage actively in public affairs. If he does, he will be torn between the duties of State and demands of the life of thought. Ordinarily he will be cautious and painstaking rather than bold and decisive. He will feel somewhat more at home in the library, the study, the laboratory, or the classroom than in the chambers of government.

But in a democratic society his ideas and his counsel will be actively sought. His thoughts will have great influence in helping not only to set standards, to establish new hypotheses, to look more deeply into and behind theories and facts, but also to make decisions. On the assumption that one of the first acts of intelligence is to seek advice from those who know, the administrators, the working committees, and the public forums of a democratic society will always weigh carefully the advice of its intellectual leaders. Their books and reports will be read and discussed, perhaps not with full comprehension, but with attention and to great advantage. Calmer and wiser heads might not always prevail, but in the give and take of democratic process the final decision will, at least, be a better decision because the men of thought have helped to formulate it. The voice of the man of thought might well be crucial in the decision-making process even though he actually had only one vote and even though the group or society might not have fully understood his principles or his reasoning. There is always the chance in a democratic society that a good idea will be totally rejected, but if so it will be freely and openly rejected and it will come up again for further consideration.

The intellectual remains a citizen. Much as he might want to detach himself—to rise above all systems and even to denationalize himself—in the interest of objective and universal truth such dreams are utopian. They are irresponsible as long as man remains a political animal and this will be as long as he remains man. As a citizen, the intellectual cannot divorce himself from the political realities any more than he can divorce himself from the realities of birth, family, and tradition. He has loyalties toward the State and these loyalties are just as valid as his loyalties toward truth, thought, and theory.

The intellectual, whether theologian, philosopher, scientist, or artist, holds an ambiguous position with regard to society or any particular group in society. He may be right and the group wrong; or he may be wrong and the group right. He may be wrong yet able to persuade the group he is right. He may be right but unable to win the support of the group. The whole question at issue may be one in which there is no right or wrong but only better or worse alternatives. Furthermore, a right or good decision at one time or under one set of circumstances might not be right or good at another time or under different circumstances. Since political power and intellectual power are seldom synonymous, there is never absolute certainty about which way the decision will go. All the intellectual can do—and this he must do—is work to bring the decision into as close an accord with the best information and the best thinking as possible.

The pursuit of excellence. Education in modern democracy finds itself confronted with a monumental task. It seeks nothing less, through its programs of universal and continuing education, than to raise the entire level of culture within the republic or democracy it serves. And education cannot be unmindful of the international and worldwide implications of its local and particularized efforts. What is involved, of course, is a frontal attack on the problem of how to upgrade the quality of life and education for all citizens without lowering the standards and meanings of excellence. Does universal education really mean inferior or second-rate education for all or is there some way of putting genuine quality into all education? It goes without saying that the fact he is in school does not necessarily guarantee the pupil a good education.

The term *pursuit of excellence* has entered into educational thinking and literature as a kind of keynote to this whole discussion. On the one hand, the term sets the ideal toward which all education should strive. On the other, it bespeaks the fear that modern education, because of a leveling process which is presumed to be at work in all democracies, can easily lose sight of that ideal. Applied to education, the pursuit of excellence means that every school and every student should try to be as good as it can possibly be. To be good is not good enough, if it is possible to be better. The desire, urge, or compulsion to be excellent, to be the best, is written large in the history of Western thought, though it has no exact counterpart in Oriental thinking.[1]

Whatever its source, the idea or ideal of pursuing excellence, as an ingredient of all educational effort, is valid and important if properly understood and qualified. Though in ordinary usage *excellence* is most often a comparative term, it is much more meaningful to think of excellence as measured against some objective criterion. As a comparative term, *excellence* is restrictive. It can be applied only to the best in each category. It is a contradiction in terms to say, on a comparative basis, that all members of a category are excellent. But it is possible to say that all the members of a category possess excellence in relation to an objective criterion. Only one runner can win the race and in so doing excel the other

---

[1] The Greeks in classical times, for example, used the word *areté* to mean that in a thing which gives it its highest virtue or excellence. The whole concept of Greek education was based on the seeking and acquiring of *areté*.

runners, for example, though all the runners in that race may be excellent runners.

The term *excellence* in this context must be qualified by the word *pursuit*. There is no person and no institution that cannot pursue excellence, that cannot try to be better. *To pursue,* here, means *to seek* or *to strive after.* There is a kind of excellence in the simple pursuit of excellence even though one may never achieve it in comparison with others. The criterion then becomes not the achievement of any particular level of accomplishment but the very effort toward excellence. Excellence is thus measured against capacity to excel. Everyone can be excellent to the extent that he pursues excellence and in so doing fulfills his own possibilities and capabilities.

In a democracy, then, the schools and the educational system should pursue excellence and strive for it. Their objective is to make it possible for all students to be excellent in fulfilling their individual capacities and in constantly stretching for higher and better goals. Those with greater capacities should be urged and inspired to go as far as they can go. The criterion for them is within themselves, an inner imperative, and not in comparison with others.

In this sense the educational pursuit of excellence is meaningful in a democracy. It is open to all. Whether education in the various democracies in the modern world is really striving for excellence is a factual question. The point here is that education in a democracy can meaningfully strive for excellence for all and in so doing it can give both dignity and depth to education in that democracy.

Part of the problem is the misunderstanding of the meaning of *excellence.* It is of small and transitory importance, except perhaps for propaganda purposes, whether some of the American schools and some of the American students, for example, excel some of the Russian schools and students or vice versa. The genuine and lasting question is whether all students in the democracies are being provided with the opportunity to understand the meaning of excellence, to pursue it as a means of fulfilling themselves and their society, and whether, under the guidance of teachers who themselves are pursuing excellence, the students will see the value in so doing.

CHAPTER VIII

Education for the Future

One of the primary functions of education in any society, but especially in a democratic one, is to look to the future and to prepare well for it. Both education and the society of the future will be faced with the problems of bigness and possible depersonalization, of rapid change, of new patterns of thought, of the peaceful uses of nuclear energy and more leisure time, of more knowledge and a smaller world. There is no indication of any kind that the presently growing emphasis on education will be reversed. On the contrary, the indications are all that the momentum will continue. Expansion in both the quantity and quality of education is to be expected. More people will be going to school, they will be in school longer, they will be specializing more deeply, and they will be actively and even formally continuing their education throughout their adult lives.

In the underdeveloped and emerging countries, an education explosion is already taking place. In these countries the desire for education is as great as the need for it. The hope of these peoples is that education will be the means for bringing them rapidly into some kind of balance with the leading countries of the world. They seek to be able to become more fully a part of the modern world. It has been said that some of the underdeveloped countries are leaping into the twentieth century without having experienced the developments of the preceding three or four centuries. This situation creates both untold opportunities and genuine problems for education.

The need for more and better education is in many ways a product of the times. At the same time that life is becoming so intricate and complex, knowledge is multiplying in every field and its scope has already reached unprecedented proportions. The most learned of men three centuries ago could not have known, for example, the science now available in an elementary school science book. Relatively simple and uncomplicated societies do not require the kind or amount of education required by advanced societies. To be part of the modern world, however, and to make a contribution to it, every person must be as fully educated as possible. Education is the only hope man has for coming to grips with the twentieth century and for finding fulfillment in it. It seems logical to assume that the future will be more and more knowledge-centered and that more and more areas of human life will be brought under rational control.

Education, in and for the future, will be crucially important. It's importance lies, at least in part, in that it provides one of the major means by which a man can engage in his time and also be saved from it. This seeming paradox involves the quality of the education of the future. The time is long since past when any one man could master all available knowledge. It is now most unlikely that any man can fully master all the knowledge available in any one of the disciplines or any one of their major subdivisions. The proliferation of knowledge leads to, and demands, intensive specialization in ever smaller and more specific areas.

The paradox is that as knowledge and life generally become more specialized, man is in danger of losing his *wholeness* or, in the literal meaning of the word, his *integrity*. At certain levels education has no choice other than to become highly specialized. But as specialization proceeds, a man could well become—again, quite literally —a machinist, or an architect, or a physicist, and fail to realize he is first and foremost a man with a dignity and destiny quite independent of, and superior to, his work within his specialized field. As specialists, it becomes more and more difficult for men to see things in their broader perspectives, their various interrelationships, and their more ultimate meanings and purposes.

In a democracy education itself is one of the major means for solving the dilemma of what might be called the dehumanization of man—i.e., the problem of overspecialization in specific subject matters to the point that human concerns become secondary. At the same time that education frankly avows the need for specialists of all kinds—not only to meet the threats and competition of other forms of government but also to further knowledge and improve the human condition—it must make sure that it strengthens the education of man as man. Specialization makes sense only if it contributes to man's fuller and higher life, not if it destroys it.

Furthermore, one is able to specialize more significantly if he has had a broad and solid background in all the areas of man's knowledge and development. Education would do well to make sure that in the course of his mature educational career, every man has the opportunity to study the profound and integrating principles of theology, the broad wisdom of philosophy, the probings of the human spirit in literature, poetry, and the fine arts, and the methods and theories of the natural and social sciences.

Education is not the only force at work in society seeking to prevent the dehumanization of man. Religion is another. Knowledge and religion have been called the twin pillars of civilization and culture. They are, indeed, twin pillars and, as such, they are not in any way incompatible. A spiritually rich and lasting civilization cannot stand on one alone. Education should not be so preoccupied with knowledge that it neglects or ignores religion. In fact, religion is, in part, a form of knowledge and education is incomplete without it.

Leadership and Public Service

As education looks to the future and takes steps to prepare itself and the society it serves for that future, it runs squarely into the question of leadership and public service in a democracy. It is clear that democracy gives rise to its own leaders. They do not become leaders by divine appointment, by fact of birth, or by military might. It is also clear that, at all levels, public service is necessary for carrying out democracy's work. The question, of course, is how to educate for leadership and how to attract both well-qualified and dedicated people into public service. Although, in a democracy, there is constant interplay between leaders and followers and the roles change frequently, the fact remains that democracy will have leaders. They will be intelligent and adept or they will be emotional, self-seeking, and inept—but they will be leaders. A democracy rests heavily on those who are willing to devote time and talent to the public interest and the public service rather than to their own private interests or for their private good.

Leadership. In a democracy, leadership takes many forms and expresses itself in many ways. The various phases of democratic life require different kinds of leadership ability. The intellectual leaders in society are not necessarily the leaders, for example, in business, in the fine arts, or in the military establishment. Leadership in a democracy is much more diffused and widespread than it would be in a society in which a central authority rules over even such matters as what is good music or art and what is good genetic theory.

The broad meaning of leadership is simply that some one person or some group of persons sets the pace and the tone, gives direction, supplies the ideas and the inspiration, controls the power, and bears the responsibility. Leadership may be formal, as when a man is elected to public office or holds an office by appointment, or it may be informal, as when a man controls the direction and action of a group by force of his ideas or personality. Leadership may be natural or acquired; it may be actively pursued by a person or it may be almost automatically bestowed on him by the group of which he is part. Genuine leadership can, of course, too, be in either a good or bad direction, and by its very nature, leadership by one or some, implies followership by the many.

Every society and every organization is only as good as its leaders, but democracy particularly depends on building an increasing supply of intelligent, experienced, and public-spirited leaders in every area of democratic life. The problem for education in a democracy revolves around the question of how to spot and encourage potential leadership ability without conflicting with the idea, so much a part of democratic theory, that all persons are to be treated equally. For an extreme example, the idea that there should be separate schools for potential leaders would be regarded by many as undemocratic. But at the other extreme, no theorists of democratic education holds that the developing of good leaders for democracy can happen just by chance. There would seem to be general agreement that in between these two extremes, education and the schools can and should be highly influential in bringing to the fore leadership ability and the genuine desire to assume leadership. More and more, educators are becoming conscious of the need to educate directly for leadership rather than to trust to good fortune that it will arise indirectly as a by-product. Those with leadership ability must be taught how to exercise it democratically, and it must be made clear to them that leadership both has high rewards and requires great sacrifices. There is increasing fear that democracy cannot produce enough good leaders because of the leveling process at work in it and because many potentially good leaders do not want to get involved.

Public service. Closely related to the problem of education for general leadership in a democracy is the problem of education for public service. In this context, *public service* does not mean the routine services of public agencies. It means more specifically the whole work of what is classically and properly called *politics.* Just as the leaders in a democracy must put the interests of the whole society above their personal interests, so, too, must those who engage in carrying on the public work of the society come to understand the public nature of their trust. As the work of free and independent human beings, politics is particularly important in a democracy. Public service is integral, indispensable, and of highest value to democratic society; it should be of first quality and should attract the nation's best people. In a democracy it should be regarded as a crowning honor to serve the people.

Part of the problem of educating for public service and of attracting good people into politics stems from one of the essential features of democracy itself: the process of election. Since election to public office depends on winning the votes of the electorate, elections can degenerate into popularity contests. The candidate must know how to please the people and he must be careful not to make enemies. This effort to please usually involves many kinds of things not directly related to the work to be done. It has been said, for example, that no man of strong ideas could ever be elected President of the United States. He must be middle-of-the-road on enough issues to get the votes to win. The hazards of the campaign and the uncertainty of the outcome keep many otherwise very good men from entering the field of politics.

Education in the democracies of the future has the twofold task of winning and preparing qualified men for politics and public service and of bringing all citizens to a realization of their function in the political field.

Intercultural Education

The great increase in travel and in speed of communication, the expansion of business markets, the heightening of international political tensions, and the general drawing closer together of the nations of the world have served to make education aware of what has heretofore been one of its most serious weaknesses. In the past, for the most part, education had tended to confine itself to studying the particular culture which was nearest at hand and which it happened to serve. Those who were educated in the United States, for example, studied Western and European culture and civilization but they knew little, if anything, about the Orient, about Africa, or even about Latin America. The reverse was true, as well: students in China or India, for example, learned very little about Western civilization. The modern age has introduced a world dimension in all thinking and has pointed to the need for strong programs in intercultural education.

It might be argued that, one hundred years ago, there was not so much need for intercultural education. Peoples from one culture rarely saw or contacted peoples from another. Now that situation has drastically changed. Intercultural education is a growing necessity of everyday life as well as a significant and valid part of educational planning. To have come to understand and appreciate the cultures of other peoples would, of course, have been a valid aspect of the educational curriculum at any time in history. To limit educational concern to one's own culture is a restriction that cannot ever be justified in educational theory. But in the modern world and the world of the future, intercultural education might also be one of the primary ways of securing the peace and putting an end to the international tensions and conflicts that arise from mutual suspicion, distrust, and misunderstanding.

The meaning of intercultural education. The broad term *culture* covers those conditions, sets of ideas and attitudes and traditions, modes of thinking and living, underlying assumptions, motivations, and criteria of proof which constitute the fundamentals of a people's way of life. The study of culture attempts to explain what peoples do and think by discovering the key concepts that identify their culture and make it unified and meaningful to them. In itself the study of culture is nonevaluative, though no study can ever be completely so. At this stage, the study of culture is comparative and informative in that it seeks to find both differences and similarities among the various cultures of the world.

The student of culture, the culturologist, is interested, among many other things, in such questions as: What are the dominant religious beliefs and practices and how do practices relate to beliefs? What are the principal values of the people? Who are the heroes and saints and sages? What is the relation between the individual and society? What are the attitudes of the people toward the family, toward education, toward work? Where does authority reside? How do changes in society come about and do these changes take place rapidly or slowly? What is the structure of the language? What are the problems with which the people most concern themselves? What is regarded as beautiful or ugly and why?

Such questions are quite clearly human or humanistic questions. But they are questions which can be legitimately asked of every culture. The answers are the bases of intercultural education.

Mathematical systems and the principles of the physical and natural sciences tend to be objective and universal in character. Though they may be valued more highly and pursued more vigorously in one culture than in another, yet they do not substantively differ from one culture to another. They are said to be transcultural or supracultural. Since one of the main obstacles to intercultural education is the language barrier, many people feel the best place to start a program of intercultural education is in the fields of mathematics and physical science, which have a "language" of their own. If so, the study moves forward to those questions whose answers are grounded in differing religious, philosophical, and sociological interpretations.

Intercultural education, then, is the means by which the available knowledge about one culture is made known in another and all others. It can be done, and is being done, in a number of ways. The exchange of professors and students from one culture or country to another on a temporary basis has proven to be highly effective. The so-called area programs of colleges and universities are becoming more numerous. Scholars from one culture often spend years studying other cultures so that their findings and interpretations can be both reported back to the students and scholars in their native cultures, and checked as well by the scholarly community of the host culture. The Peace Corps program is an important experiment in intercultural education. UNESCO, a special agency of the United Nations, is doing much good work in this field. But much more needs to be done and whole areas of culture still remain unexplored.

The purpose of intercultural education.   Intercultural education is a valid and necessary form of intellectual discipline in and of itself. To establish itself as part of the curriculum or as part of a continuing education program, it needs no other justification than the fact that it adheres to all the principles governing the pursuit of knowledge and the teaching of it. If the principal study of man is man, there is no good reason for limiting the study of man to the study of man in his own cultural setting.

But intercultural education fulfills an important purpose over and above this. It serves to create mutual understanding among the peoples of the world. It provides a basis on which peoples can come to know, respect, and appreciate one another. It supplies the framework within which discussion can take place, stereotypes can be eliminated, and new approaches to cooperation can be worked out. It helps to allay fears arising out of misunderstood intentions and sensitivities. It creates bonds of friendship. But it also, if needs be, brings to the surface the information by which one can know his enemy and know how to deal with him intelligently.

Intercultural education, in its present stage of development, aims at knowledge and appreciation. In itself it does not seek to set standards of superiority and inferiority. Its aim is not to suggest and impose changes. Each culture has a right to its own principles and ways of doing things. Diversity of culture can be enriching, and a world democracy can embrace diversity just as a national democracy can. But it is not inconceivable that from extended programs of intercultural education there might emerge patterns of participation and cooperation which, at least in the practical order, would lead to greater world unity and world peace. Such programs might well be a major factor in determining whether the countries of the world, and the world society of the future, will be ruled by *the one, the few,* or *the many.*

Bibliography

Appleby, Paul H., *Big Democracy*. New York: Alfred A. Knopf, 1945.

Aristotle, *Politics*.

Brecht, Arnold, *Political Theory; The Foundations of Twentieth-Century Political Thought*. Princeton, N.J.: Princeton University Press, 1959.

Curtis, Michael (Ed.), *The Nature of Politics*. New York: Avon Book Division of The Hearst Corporation, 1962.

DeGrazia, Alfred and Thomas H. Stevenson, *World Politics*. New York: Barnes & Noble, Inc., 1962.

Dewey, John, *Democracy and Education*. New York: The Macmillan Company, 1916.

Donlan, O. P., Thomas C., *Theology and Education*. Dubuque, Iowa: William C. Brown Company, Publishers, 1952.

Hook, Sidney, *Political Power and Personal Freedom*. New York: Criterion Books, Inc., 1959.

Houle, Cyril O. and Charles A. Nelsen, *The University, The Citizen, and World Affairs*. Washington, D.C.: American Council on Education, 1956.

Jaeger, Werner, *Paideia: The Ideals of Greek Culture*. New York: Oxford University Press, 1943. Translated by Gilbert Highet. 3 vols.

Lippmann, Walter, *The Public Philosophy*. New York: New American Library of World Literature, Inc., Copyright 1955 Walter Lippmann. Published as a Mentor Book. First Printing, May, 1956.

Mannheim, Karl, *Ideology and Utopia*. New York: Harcourt, Brace & World, Inc., 1952.

Maritain, Jacques, *The Person and the Common Good*. New York: Charles Scribner's Sons, 1947. Translated by John J. Fitzgerald.

———, *True Humanism*. New York: Charles Scribner's Sons, 1938. Translated by M. R. Adamson.

Northrup, F. S. C., *Ideological Differences and World Order*. New Haven: Yale University Press, 1949.

Plato, *The Republic*.

Rommen, Heinrich A., *The Natural Law*. St. Louis, Mo.: B. Herder Book Co., 1947. Translated by Thomas R. Hanley.

St. Thomas Aquinas, *Selected Political Writings*. Edited and with Introduction by A. P. D'Entréves. Oxford: B. Blackwell, 1948. Translated by J. G. Dawson.

Simon, Ives, *The Philosophy of Democratic Government*. Chicago: University of Chicago Press, 1951.

Snow, C. P., *The Two Cultures and the Scientific Revolution*. New York: Cambridge University Press, 1959.

Voegelin, Eric, *The New Science of Politics, An Introduction*. Chicago: University of Chicago Press, 1952.

Index

Index

A

Abilities, individual, 67
Action, 93
Aquinas, Thomas, 2
Areté, 97
Aristocracy, 6, 20
  advantages of, 21
  of blood, 22
  disadvantages of, 21
  and ideology, 24
  of intelligence, 23
  of military might, 23
  of wealth, 23
Aristotle, 2, 5, 8, 34
Authority, 5, 35

C

Change, and creativity, 81
Charlemagne, 12
Child, the, 49
Church and State, separation of, 92
Citizen, the, 35, 42
Civilization, 57
Coercion, 68
Cold War, the, 38
Common Good, the, 41, 43
Communism, 7
  atheism, 26
  Communist Party, 7, 25
  as an economic system, 39
  ideology, 29
Compromise, 57
Constitution, basis of political systems,
  2
Constitutionalism, 60
Cooperation, essential to democracy, 41
Creativity, 81ff
Criticism, self, 79
Culture, 57
Curriculum, 17, 31, 81
  defined, 17
  methods of teaching, 18, 32

D

Democracy:
  bases of, 54

Democracy (*Cont.*)
  conditions for survival, 39
  as content, 59, 65
  decision-making power, 35
  democratic charter, 60
  principles of, 38
  as process, 59
Dewey, John, 44
Dictatorship, 6
Dignity, human, 55

E

Education:
  compulsory, 15
  financing of, 27
  formal, 9ff
  general, 63
  informal, 9ff
  intercultural, 103ff
  liberal, 63, 64
  meaningfulness in, 50
  private, 87
  public, 87
  purpose of, 43
  quality of, 14, 30, 49
  quantity of, 14, 30, 40, 48
  specialized, 64
  teachers' 16
  theory of, 81
  universal, 15
Elite, the, 21
Emotions, 57
Environment, 82
Equity, 75
Evaluation, 79
Excellence, 97ff
Experience, 56

F

Faith, 54
Field Theory, 1
Founding fathers, the, 68
Freedom, 56, 59
  academic, 78
  of inquiry, 77
  meaning of, 52
  ontological, 62
  operational, 62

G

God, 6, 35
Government, 36

I

Ideas, 51
Individual, the, 41
  differences in, 71
  dignity of, 70
  the good of, 42
  as a person, 42
Indoctrination, 26, 28, 70
Integration, racial, 85
Integrity, of education, 85ff
Intellectual, the, 95ff
Intellectual honesty, 52
Intelligence, general, 82

J

Jaeger, Werner, 74
Jefferson, Thomas, 39
Judgment, 57

L

Law, the, 60
Leadership, 37, 101ff
Learning, climate of, 53
Learning by doing, 66
Legislation, 67
Liberation, 63
Liberty, 62
Lincoln, Abraham, 40

M

Majority, rights of, 61
Man, 2
  Christian concept of, 35
  essentially a political animal, 2
Maritan, Jacques, 2, 47, 48
Method, scientific, 62
Minority, rights of, 61
"Mobocracy," 7
Monarchy, 6

O

Oligarchy, 6

Opportunity, equal, 73
Ortega y Gasset, J., 16
Oregon School Case, 88

P

Paideia, 64
Parents:
  In loco parentis, 89
  rights of, 89
Participation, in the democratic process, 61
Personality, cult of, 14
Pius XI, Pope, 44
Politics, 2
Political organizations, modes of, 9
Political systems, 3ff
Principle, 86
Property, 59
Public service, 101ff

R

Reason, 56
Republic, 36
Rights, individual, 60
Rousseau, Jean Jacques, 5
Rule, 5
  defined, 5
  by the few, 5
  by the many, 5
  by the one, 5
  in the public interest, 6
  not in the public interest, 6

S

Schooling, 81
Schools, 66
Sectioning, 72
Self-expression, 67
Simon, Yves, 5
Snow, C. P., 46
Society, open, 52
Socrates, 78
State, the, 8
  and education, 8
  and political systems, 8

T

Taxation, 91
Teacher, the, 16

Teacher (*Cont.*)
  as cooperative artist, 71
  as mediator, 51
  personal relationships with students,
    51
  preparation of, 16
  role in a democracy, 50
  and society, 52
Teaching, 18
  how to think, 51
  Logical–Psychological, 18
  methods of, rule by the one, 18
  what to think, 51
Tutor, 87

U

UNESCO, 38

V

Values, 47
Vote, the, 37, 67
Voting, 46

W

Wisdom, 53